180 DAYS™

Phonics

for Prekindergarten

T0357842

Author

Sarah Massie, M.Ed.

Consultant

Lisa Hollis, M.A.Ed.
First Grade Teacher
Sylvan Union School District

Publishing Credits

Corinne Burton, M.A.Ed., *President* and *Publisher*
Gabe Thibodeau, *Content Director*
Véronique Bos, *VP of Creative*
Lynette Ordoñez, *Content Manager*
Jill Malcolm, *Senior Graphic Designer*

Image Credits: all images from Shuttertock and/or iStock

Standards

A division of Teacher Created Materials
5482 Argosy Avenue
Huntington Beach, CA 92649
www.tcmpub.com/shell-education
ISBN 978-1-0876-6254-1

Printed by: 51497
Printed in: China

Table of Contents

Introduction

180 Days of Practice

Appendix

What Is Phonics?

Learning to read is a complex process. Students must know the speech sounds associated with written letters in words, how to put those sounds together to form pronounceable words, and how to recognize words rapidly (Beck and Beck 2013). Phonics is a method of instruction that teaches learners the relationship between sounds and letters and how to use those sounds and letters to read and spell. Practice is especially important to help early readers recognize words rapidly. *180 Days™: Phonics* offers teachers and parents a full page of targeted phonics practice activities for each day of the school year.

The Science of Reading

Phonics instruction has historically been at the forefront of much debate and research. The "whole-language" approach presented in the *Dick and Jane* books dominated beginning reading instruction with its "look-say" method that required students to memorize whole words without paying any attention to decoding (sounding out) words. This method was highly criticized by Rudolf Flesch's 1955 publication *Why Johnny Can't Read* and by Jeanne Chall's 1967 publication *Learning to Read: The Great Debate*. Both researchers indicated the need for direct phonics instruction in place of teaching trial and error and the memorization of whole words. In 1997, Congress commissioned a review of this reading research. The National Reading Panel (NRP) released their report in 2000, which became the backbone of the Science of Reading. The panel's findings clearly showed that, for students to become better readers, they need systematic and explicit instruction in these five areas:

- Phonemic Awareness: understanding and manipulating individual speech sounds
- Phonics: matching sounds to letters for use in reading and spelling
- Fluency: reading connected text accurately and smoothly
- Vocabulary: knowing the meanings of words in speech and in print
- Reading Comprehension: understanding what is read

An effective reading program must include instruction in foundational skills, such as phonemic awareness, as well as direct instruction in relating sounds to written letters or sequences of letters that represent those sounds.

Phonics will more than likely continue to play a key role in the Science of Reading. Decades of research have proven it to be the most effective means for building foundational literacy in learners.

What Is Phonics? *(cont.)*

Elements of Instruction

The alphabetic principle is the idea that letters and letter patterns represent the sounds of spoken language. When students who are learning to read and write begin to connect letters (graphemes) with their sounds (phonemes), they have cracked the alphabetic principle. The goal of phonics instruction is to teach students that there are systematic and predictable relationships between written letters and spoken sounds. Learning these predictable relationships helps students apply the alphabetic principle to both familiar and unfamiliar words and to begin to read with fluency.

Children use their prior learning as a bridge to new learning. For this reason, the best phonics instruction presents skills sequentially from simple to complex. According to Robert Marzano, "Practice has always been, and always will be, a necessary ingredient to learning procedural knowledge at a level at which students execute it independently" (2010, 83). Practice is especially important to help students apply phonics concepts to a wide range of words. Learners need multiple opportunities to review learned skills and to practice the relationship between letters and sound patterns.

Research to Practice

180 Days™: Phonics has been informed by reading research. This series provides opportunities for students to practice the skills that are proven to contribute to reading growth.

- Phonics concepts are presented from **simple to complex** with prior learning embedded within each week. This provides students with **multiple opportunities to practice** target skills.
- Daily practices intentionally build upon one another to help students **bridge new learning** to prior concepts.
- Specific **language comprehension** and **word-recognition skills** are reinforced throughout the activities.
- An overview page is provided before each unit to introduce key concepts and provide **explicit instructional strategies**.
- **Phonemic awareness** and **phonological awareness** are embedded within the progression of skills and concepts.
- Students read and write words with target concepts to reinforce the connection between **graphemes** and **phonemes**.

How to Use This Resource

Unit Structure Overview

This resource is divided into 7 units. Each unit focuses on a specific phonics concept. This provides ample practice with each concept before moving on to more complex patterns.

Unit	Week	Focus
Unit 1: Concepts of Print	Weeks 1–4	Concept of a Letter First and Last Letter One-to-One Match Concept of a Word
Unit 2: Short *Aa*	5	Short *Aa*
	6	Consonant *Mm*
	7	Consonant *Tt*
	8	Consonant *Ss*
	9	Consonant *Pp*
	10	Review: *Aa, Mm, Tt, Ss, Pp*
Unit 3: Short *Ii*	11	Short *Ii*
	12	Consonant *Nn*
	13	Consonant *Ff*
	14	Consonant *Gg*
	15	Consonant *Bb*
	16	Review: *Ii, Nn, Ff, Gg, Bb*
Unit 4: Short *Oo*	17	Short *Oo*
	18	Consonant *Cc*
	19	Consonant *Ll*
	20	Consonant *Hh*
	21	Consonant *Jj*
	22	Review: *Oo, Cc, Ll, Hh, Jj*

Unit	Week	Focus
Unit 5: Short *Uu*	23	Short *Uu*
	24	Consonant *Rr*
	25	Consonant *Kk*
	26	Consonant *Dd*
	27	Consonant *Yy*
	28	Review: *Uu, Rr, Kk, Dd, Yy*
Unit 6: Short *Ee*	29	Short *Ee*
	30	Consonant *Qq*
	31	Consonant *Ww*
	32	Consonant *Vv*
	33	Consonants *Xx* and *Zz*
	34	Review: *Ee, Qq, Ww, Vv, Xx, Zz*
Unit 7: Cumulative Review	Weeks 35–36	Making CVC words

How to Use This Resource *(cont.)*

Overview Pages

Each unit follows a consistent format for ease of use. An overview page introduces phonics concepts at the beginning of each unit. These pages support family understanding and provide opportunities to prepare students for the activities presented in the following practice pages. Teachers may wish to send the page home with students at the beginning of each unit to inform parents of what is being learned at school.

A box at the top of each page explains the phonics concept presented in the unit.

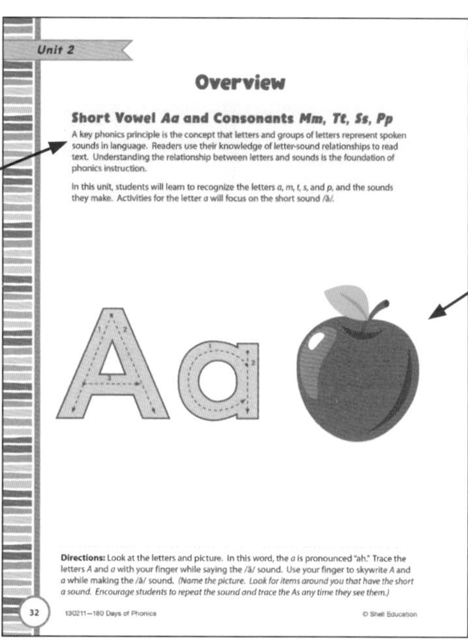

Unit 2

Overview

Short Vowel *Aa* and Consonants *Mm, Tt, Ss, Pp*

A key phonics principle is the concept that letters and groups of letters represent spoken sounds in language. Readers use their knowledge of letter-sound relationships to read text. Understanding the relationship between letters and sounds is the foundation of phonics instruction.

In this unit, students will learn to recognize the letters *a, m, t, s,* and *p,* and the sounds they make. Activities for the letter *a* will focus on the short sound /ă/.

Aa

Directions: Look at the letters and picture. In this word, the *a* is pronounced "ah." Trace the letters *A* and *a* with your finger while saying the /ă/ sound. Use your finger to skywrite *A* and *a* while making the /ă/ sound. *(Name the picture. Look for items around you that have the short a sound. Encourage students to repeat the sound and trace the As any time they see them.)*

32 130211—180 Days of Phonics © Shell Education

An introductory activity provides an example of a strategy used within the unit or addresses common misconceptions with a specific phonics skill. Complete this activity as a class or in small groups to help prepare students for the upcoming topics.

How to Use This Resource *(cont.)*

Student Practice Pages

Practice pages reinforce grade-level phonics skills. This book provides one practice page for each day of the school year. Each day's phonics activity is provided as a full practice page, making it easy to prepare and implement as part of a morning routine, at the beginning of each phonics lesson, or as homework.

Day 1 of each week teaches students the phonics focus of the week and how to identify the target sounds.

On **Days 2 and 3**, students isolate beginning, middle, or end phonemes.

On **Day 4**, students blend sounds or syllables to read words.

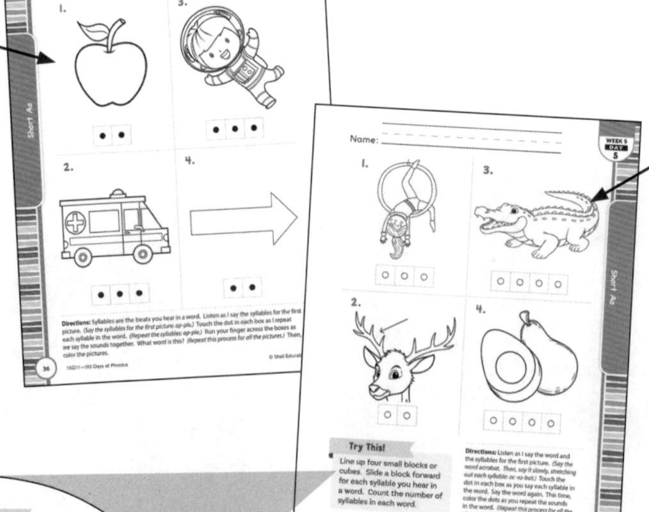

At the end of the week on **Day 5,** students segment sounds or syllables to read and write words.

Try This!

Line up four small blocks or cubes. Slide a block forward for each syllable you hear in a word. Count the number of syllables in each word.

Try This! activities are included throughout the book. They provide opportunities to practice phonics concepts through adult-led hands-on tasks.

How to Use This Resource *(cont.)*

Digital Resources

Several resources are provided digitally. (See page 214 for instructions on how to download these pages.) These tools include the following:

- **Standards Correlations**—This resource shows how the activities align with key standards.
- **Class and Individual Analysis Sheets**—These analysis sheets can be used to track student progress toward mastery of concepts. Results can be analyzed to determine next steps for differentiating instruction to meet varying student needs.
- **Hands-On Letter Practice**—These large uppercase and lowercase letters include formation arrows. This makes it the perfect tool for students to practice with their fingers or with pencils.
- **Writing Practice**—These pages include dotted uppercase and lowercase letters on writing lines.

Instructional Options

180 Days™: Phonics is a flexible resource that can be used in various instructional settings for different purposes.

- Use the practice pages as daily warm-up activities.
- Work with students in small groups, allowing them to focus on specific skills. This setting also lends itself to partner and group discussions about the phonics focus.
- Practice pages in this resource can be completed independently during center times and as activities for early finishers.

How to Use This Resource *(cont.)*

Diagnostic Assessment

The practice pages in this book can be used as diagnostic assessments. These activity pages require students to identify specific phonics concepts within words, read connected text, and write responses using target concepts. (An answer key for the practice pages is provided starting on page 201.)

Analysis sheets are provided as Microsoft Word® files in the digital resources. There is a Class Analysis Sheet and an Individual Analysis Sheet. Use the file that matches your assessment needs. At the end of a unit, count the number of problems students got correct for the last week and enter it into the chart. Analyze the data on the analysis sheet to determine instructional focuses for your child or class.

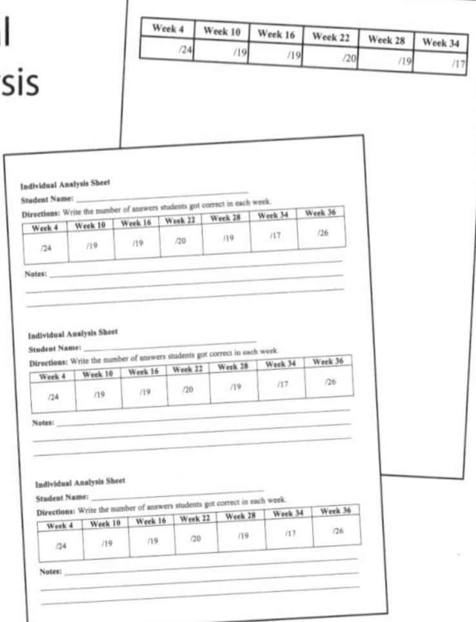

Week 4	Week 10	Week 16	Week 22	Week 28	Week 34
/24	/19	/19	/20	/19	/17

Individual Analysis Sheet

Student Name: ____________

Directions: Write the number of answers students got correct in each week.

Week 4	Week 10	Week 16	Week 22	Week 28	Week 34	Week 36
/24	/19	/19	/20	/19	/17	/26

Notes: ____________

Individual Analysis Sheet

Student Name: ____________

Directions: Write the number of answers students got correct in each week.

Week 4	Week 10	Week 16	Week 22	Week 28	Week 34	Week 36
/24	/19	/19	/20	/19	/17	/26

Notes: ____________

Individual Analysis Sheet

Student Name: ____________

Directions: Write the number of answers students got correct in each week.

Week 4	Week 10	Week 16	Week 22	Week 28	Week 34	Week 36
/24	/19	/19	/20	/19	/17	/26

Notes: ____________

The diagnostic analysis tools included in the digital resources allow for quick evaluation and ongoing monitoring of student work. They help you to quickly identify which phonics concepts students may need to explore further to develop fluency.

Using the Results to Differentiate Instruction

Once results are gathered and analyzed, use the data to inform how to differentiate instruction. The data can help determine which concepts are the most difficult for students, as well as identify the students who need additional instructional support and continued practice.

The results of the diagnostic analysis may show that an entire class is struggling with a particular phonics concept. If these concepts have been taught in the past, this indicates that further instruction or reteaching is necessary. If these concepts have not yet been taught, this data is a great preassessment tool to demonstrate students do not have a working knowledge of the concepts.

The results of the diagnostic analysis may also show that an individual or small group of students is struggling with a particular concept or group of concepts. Consider pulling aside these students to instruct further on the concept(s) while others work independently. You can also use the results to help identify individuals or groups of proficient students who are ready for enrichment or above-grade-level instruction. These students may benefit from independent learning contracts or more challenging activities.

Overview

Concepts of Print

Concepts of print are foundational skills for phonics instruction. In this unit, students will learn four key concepts of print.

Concept of a Letter: Learning to distinguish between letters, numbers, and shapes is an important step on the road to literacy.

First and Last Letters: Identifying first and last letters helps students focus on individual letters within a word.

One-to-One Match: This skill helps students understand that each written word stands for a spoken word.

Concept of a Word: Recognizing where words begin and end and how they represent spoken language is one of the first building blocks of reading.

I see a plant.

• • • •

Directions: Look at the sentence. Touch the dot under each word as I read it. Count the words in the sentence. *(Note the spaces between each word as students count. Then, read the sentence again.)* Which words are just one letter? Which words have more than one letter?

Name: ____________________

Concept of a Letter

Directions: Trace the letters *A* and *a* with your finger. Trace the letters with a crayon. Name each picture. Circle each letter. Write an *X* on each picture.

Name: ______________________

Directions: Trace each letter with your finger. Name each picture. Circle each letter. Write an *X* on each picture.

Name: ______________________

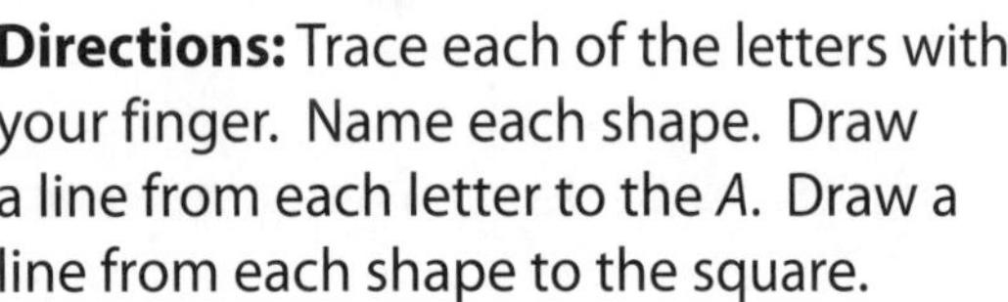

Directions: Trace each of the letters with your finger. Name each shape. Draw a line from each letter to the *A*. Draw a line from each shape to the square.

Try This!

Go on a letter hunt. See how many letters you can find around you. Write them on a sheet of paper or a whiteboard.

Name: ______________________

2

v

C

5

m

3

D

1

L

4

p

Concept of a Letter

Try This!

Look for letters and numbers in a book. Talk about where each is located and why they are there.

Directions: Trace each letter with your finger. Name each letter. Circle the letters. Write an *X* on each number.

Name: ______________________

Concept of a Letter

Tt	T			t
Bb		B	b	
Jj	J		j	
Pp		p		P
Kk	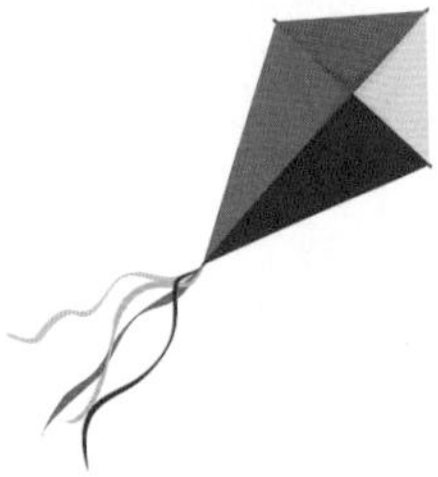	k	K	

Directions: Trace the first letters in each row with your finger. Circle the matching letters in the row. Write an *X* on each picture.

Name: ____________________

Directions: Name the picture. Touch the word. Count the letters in the word. Color the first letter in the word. Color the last letter in the word with a different color.

Name: ______________________

First and Last Letter

Directions: Draw yourself in the box. Write your name under your picture. Count the letters in your name. Circle the first letter of your name. Underline the last letter of your name.

Try This!

Make a list of your family members' names. Circle the first and last letter of each name. Look for those letters around you.

Name: ______________________

hat

tie

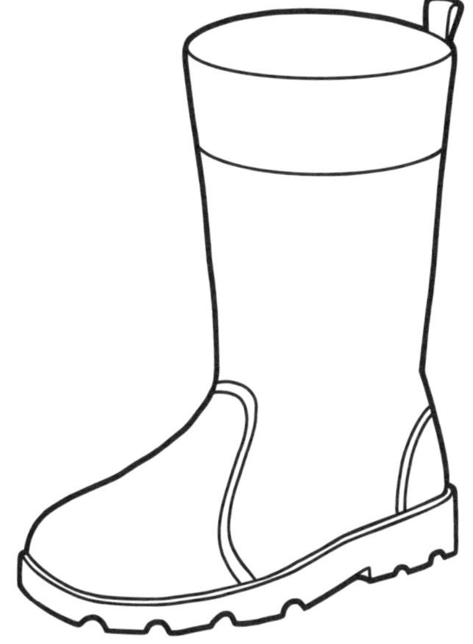

boot

sock

Directions: Name each picture. Touch each word. Count the letters in each word. Circle the first letter in each word. Then, color the pictures.

Name: ____________________

Directions: Name each picture. Touch each word. Count the letters in each word. Underline the last letter in each word. Then, color the pictures.

Try This!

Look for signs and labels around you. Trace the first and last letter in each word with your finger.

Name: ______________________

dog

fish

bird

cat

horse

frog

First and Last Letter

Directions: Name each picture. Touch each word. Count the letters in each word. Circle the first letter in each word. Underline the last letter in each word. Then, color the pictures.

Name: ______________________

One-to-One Match

Directions: Name each picture from left to right. As you name each picture, touch the dot below it. Do this two more times. Then, color the pictures.

Try This!

Line up a group of toys. Name each toy from left to right. Touch each toy as you say it.

Name: ________________

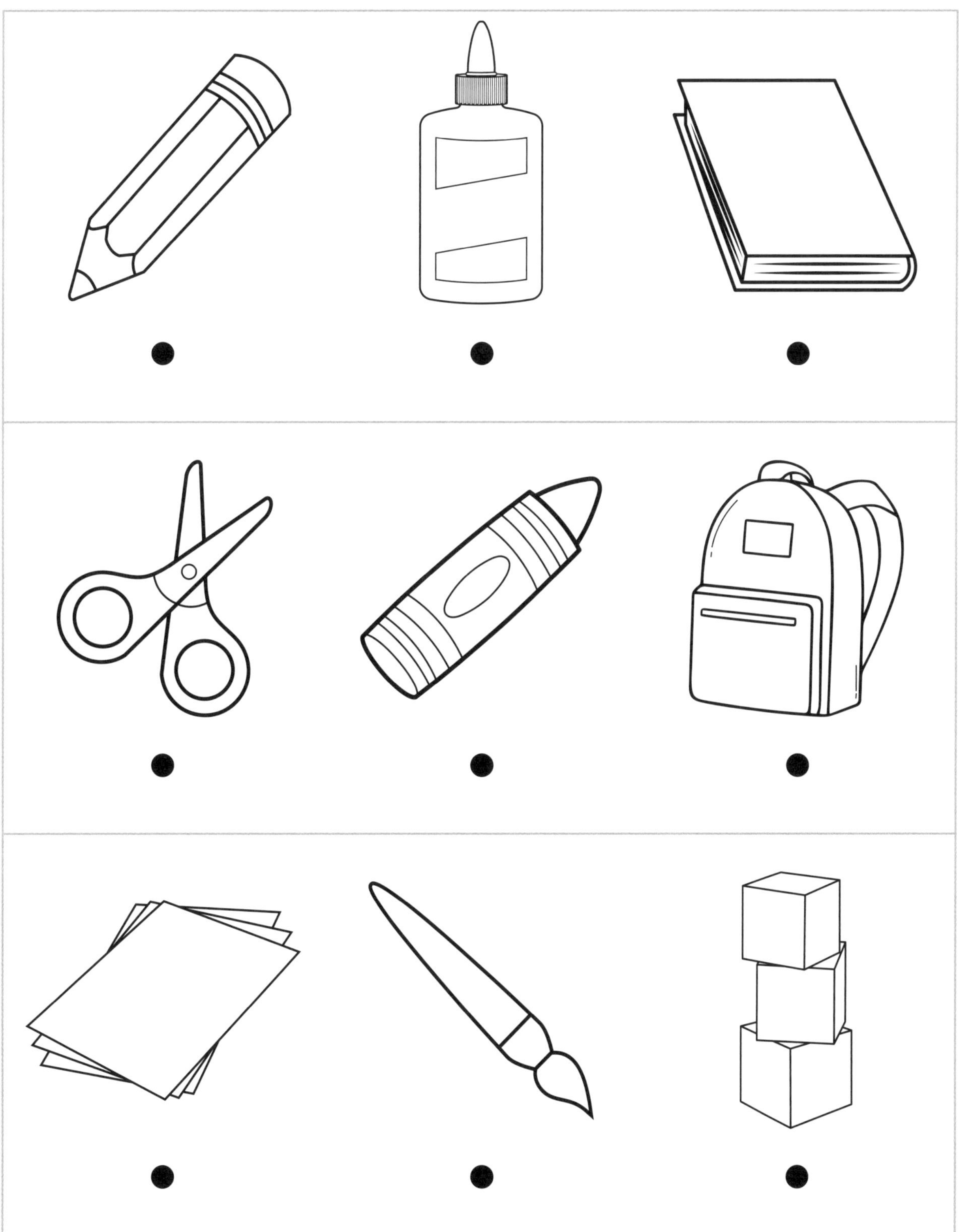

Directions: Start at the top row. Name each picture from left to right. As you name each picture, touch the dot below it. Repeat this for the second and third row. Then, color the pictures.

Name: ______________________

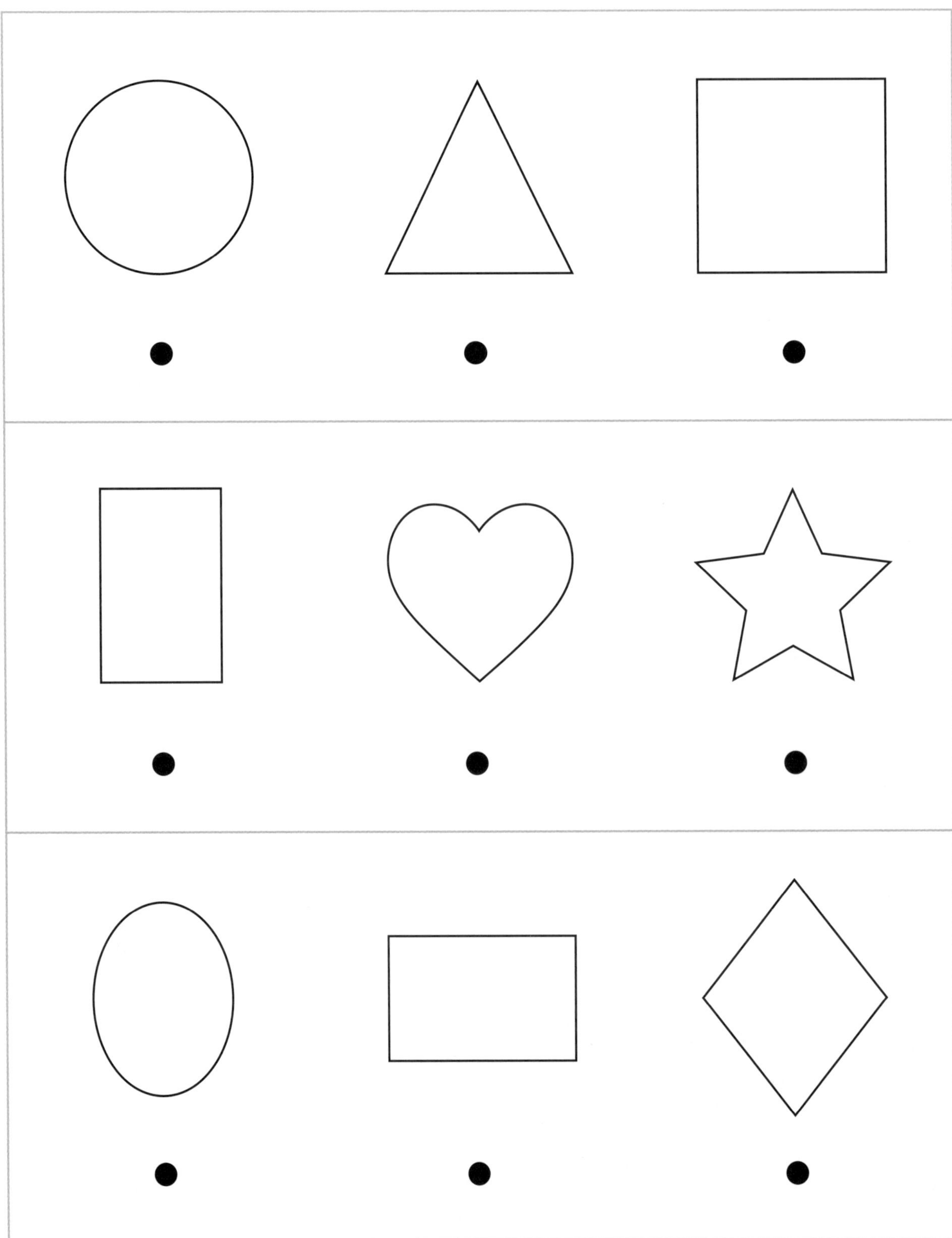

Directions: Start at the top row. Name each shape from left to right. As you name each shape, touch the dot below it. Repeat this for the second and third row. Then, color the shapes.

Name: ____________________

p	W	i	F	s
•	•	•	•	•
t	Z	b	m	K
•	•	•	•	•
R	L	v	e	C
•	•	•	•	•

One-to-One Match

Try This!

Look for words around you. When you find a word, touch each letter from left to right as an adult reads them to you.

Directions: Start at the top row. As I name each letter, touch the dot below it. Repeat this for the second and third row. *(Read each letter aloud to students as they touch the dot beneath it.)*

Name: ____________________

The apple tree is tall. It has green leaves. Flowers grow into apples. They are ready to harvest in fall.

Directions: Touch the dot below each word. As you touch each dot, I will read the word above it. Read the text twice together. *(Read each word aloud to students as they touch the dot beneath it.)*

Try This!

Practice this skill as you look at books. Touch each word as an adult reads it to you.

Name: ______________________________

Directions: Draw one thing you love in each box. Label each picture. Draw a line from each word to its picture. Say the word as you do this. *(Write one word to label each drawing the student has made.)*

Name: ____________________

bee

cup

ice

pig

e u o H

Concept of a Word

Directions: Circle the words. Trace the letters. Then, color the pictures.

Try This!

Make a word collage. Cut large words out of magazines or newspapers, and glue them onto construction paper. Draw a picture for each word you find.

Name: ______________________

boat

•

car

•

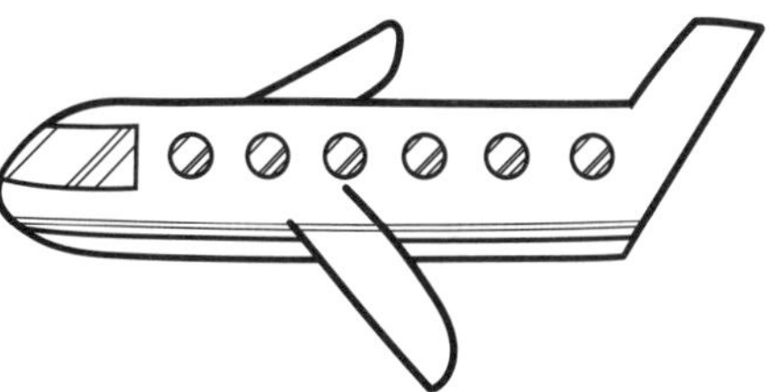

plane

•

train

•

truck

•

Directions: Touch the dot under each word. Listen closely as I read each word when you touch it. After I read each word, draw a line to connect it to the matching picture. Then, color the pictures. *(Read each word aloud, pausing for the student to find the matching picture.)*

Name: ______________________

Concept of a Word

ring •	r ring
ball •	b ball
pizza •	pizza p
crab •	c crab
net •	n net

Directions: Touch the dot under each word. Listen closely as I read each word when you touch it. After I read each word, circle the word that matches. *(Read each word aloud, pausing for the student to find the matching word.)*

Name: ______________________________

I love to read.

• • • •

1 2 3 4 5

Try This!

Search for words in your community. Count how many words you find in one trip.

Directions: Touch each word as I read the sentence. *(Read the sentence aloud as the student touches each word.)* Count the words in the sentence. Trace the matching number. Draw a line from the number to the sentence. Then, color the picture.

Overview

Short Vowel *Aa* and Consonants *Mm*, *Tt*, *Ss*, and *Pp*

A key phonics principle is the concept that letters and groups of letters represent spoken sounds in language. Readers use their knowledge of letter-sound relationships to read text. Understanding the relationship between letters and sounds is the foundation of phonics instruction.

In this unit, students will learn to recognize the letters *a*, *m*, *t*, *s*, and *p* and the sounds they make. Activities for the letter *a* will focus on the short sound /ă/.

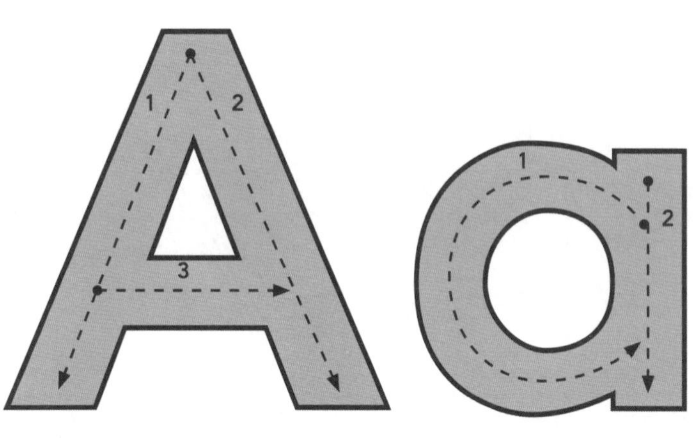

Directions: Look at the letters and picture. In this word, the *a* is pronounced "ah." Trace the letters *A* and *a* with your finger while saying the /ă/ sound. Use your finger to skywrite *A* and *a* while making the /ă/ sound. *(Name the picture. Look for items around you that have the short a sound. Encourage students to repeat the sound and trace the* As *any time they see them.)*

Name: ____________________

Directions: Trace the letters *A* and *a* with your finger while saying the sound /ă/. Repeat this sound while skywriting the letters. Name each picture, listening for the /ă/ sound. Find something around you that begins with the /ă/ sound, and draw it in the box.

Name: ______________________

Directions: Name each picture. Say the first sound you hear in each word. Circle the picture that begins with the /ă/ sound. Draw an item that begins with the /ă/ sound in the box.

Try This!

Practice writing the letters *A* and *a* with chalk. Practice the /ă/ sound each time you write the letters.

Name: ______________________

Directions: Name each picture in the table. Say the first sound you hear in each word. Circle the picture that begins with the /ă/ sound. Look at the pictures below. Color the image that begins with the /ă/ sound.

Name: ______________________

1.

● ●

3.

● ● ●

2.

● ● ●

4.

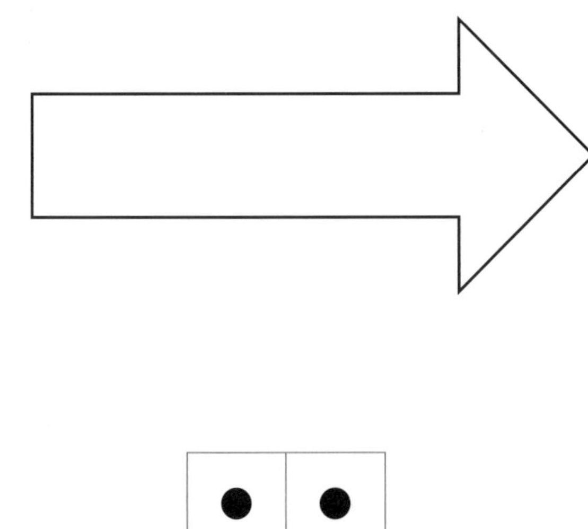

● ●

Directions: Syllables are the beats you hear in a word. Listen as I say the syllables for the first picture. *(Say the syllables for the first picture: ap-ple.)* Touch the dot in each box as I repeat each syllable in the word. *(Repeat the syllables: ap-ple.)* Run your finger across the boxes as we say the sounds together. What word is this? *(Repeat this process for all the pictures.)* Then, color the pictures.

Name: ______________________

1.

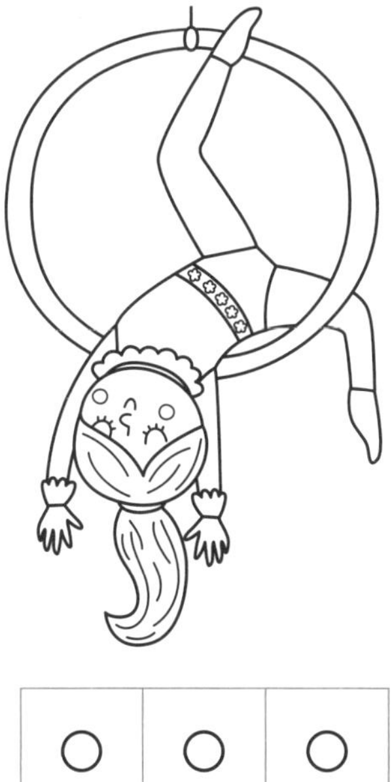

○ ○ ○

3.

○ ○ ○ ○

2.

○ ○

4.

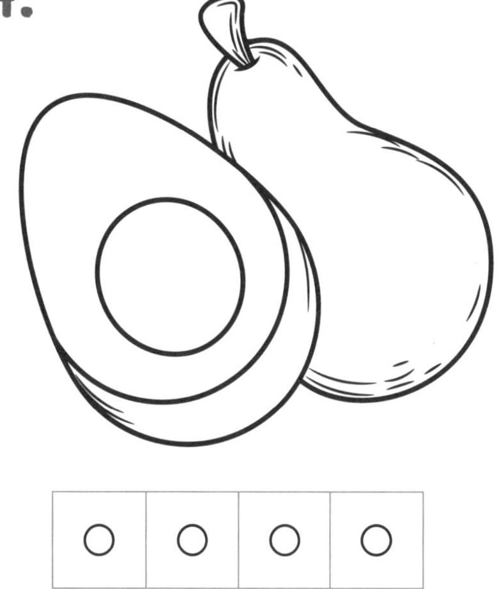

○ ○ ○ ○

Try This!

Line up four small blocks or cubes. Slide a block forward for each syllable you hear in a word. Count the number of syllables in each word.

Directions: Listen as I say the word and the syllables for the first picture. *(Say the word* acrobat. *Then, say it slowly, stretching out each syllable: ac-ro-bat.)* Touch the dot in each box as you say each syllable in the word. Say the word again. This time, color the dots as you repeat the sounds in the word. *(Repeat this process for all the pictures.)* Then, color the pictures.

Name: ____________________

mug

milk

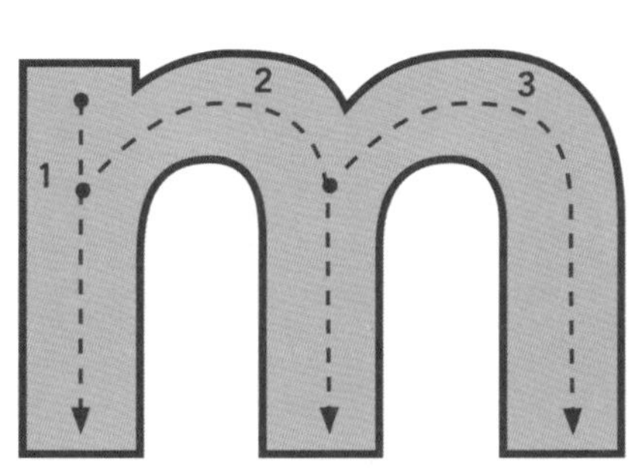

mop

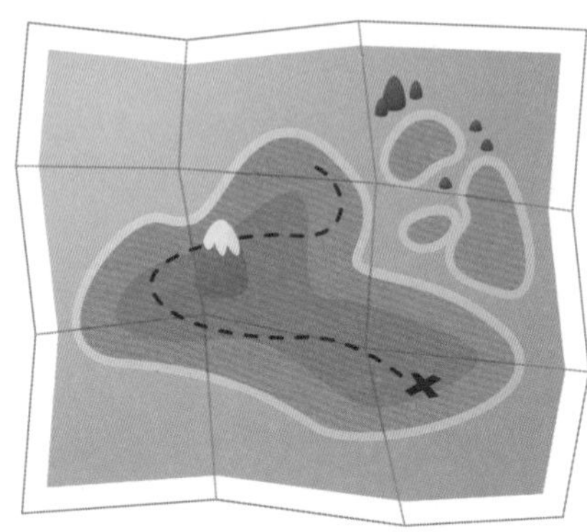

map

Directions: Trace the letters *M* and *m* with your finger while saying the sound /m/. Repeat this sound while skywriting the letters. Name each picture, listening for the /m/ sound. Find something around you that begins with the /m/ sound. Draw it in the box.

Name: ____________________

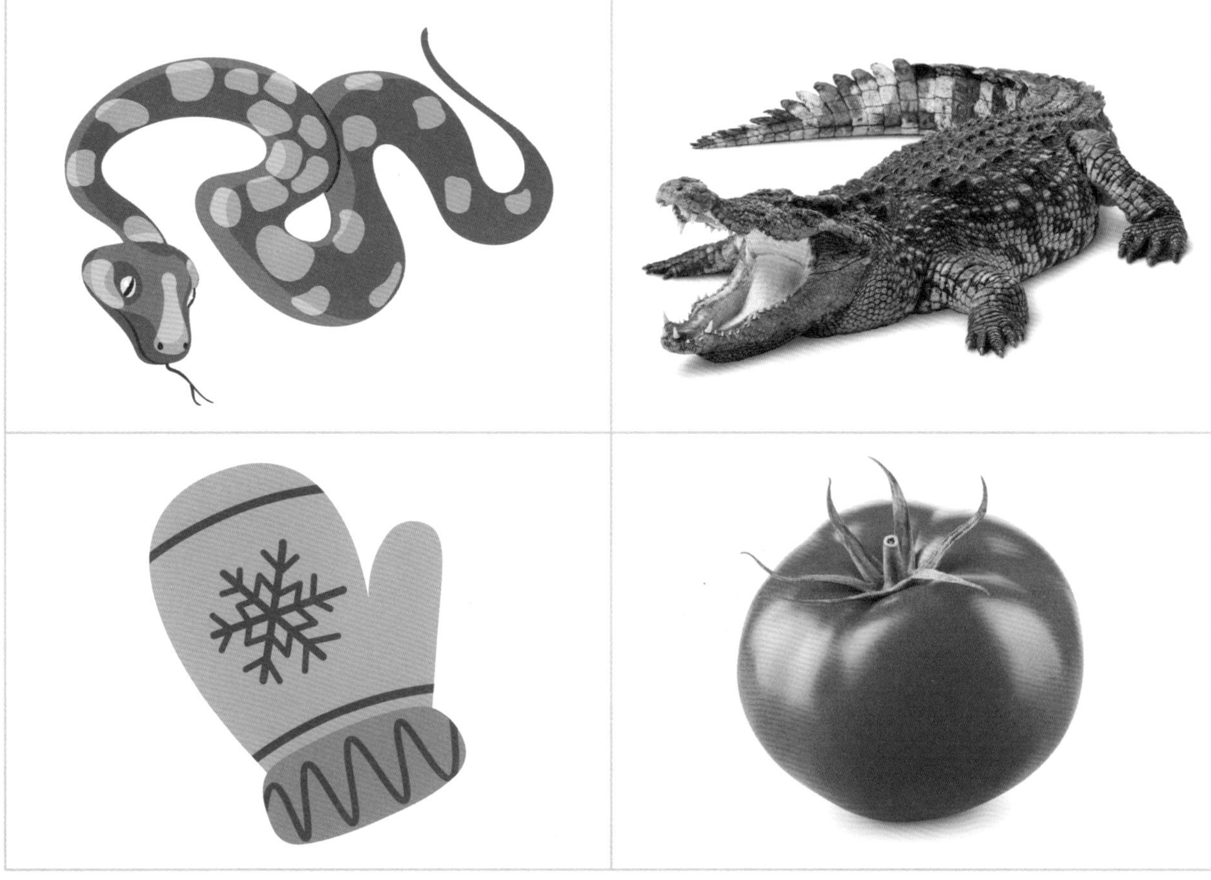

Try This!

Practice writing letters with different materials. Cover a tray or flat surface with rice, sand, or modeling clay. Then, form the letters *M* and *m* while saying /m/.

Directions: Name each picture. Say the first sound you hear in each word. Circle the picture that begins with the /m/ sound. Draw an item that begins with the /m/ sound in the box.

Name: ______________________

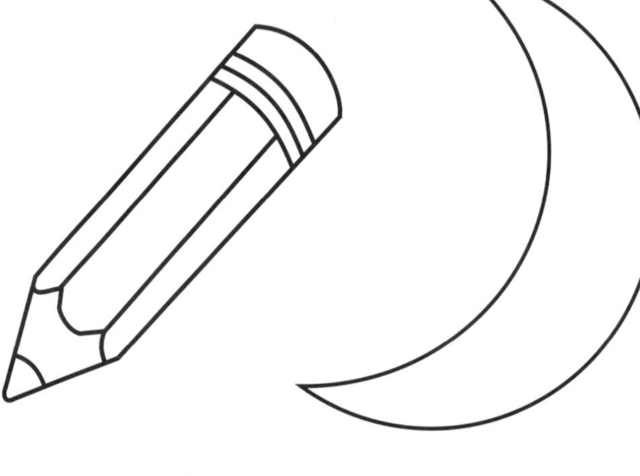

Directions: Name each picture in the table. Say the first sound you hear in each word. Circle the picture that begins with the /m/ sound. Look at the pictures below. Color the images that begin with the /m/ sound.

Try This!

Draw a plate with different foods. Say the sound you hear at the beginning of each food. Try to think of foods that start with the /m/ sound.

Name: ______________________

1.

3.

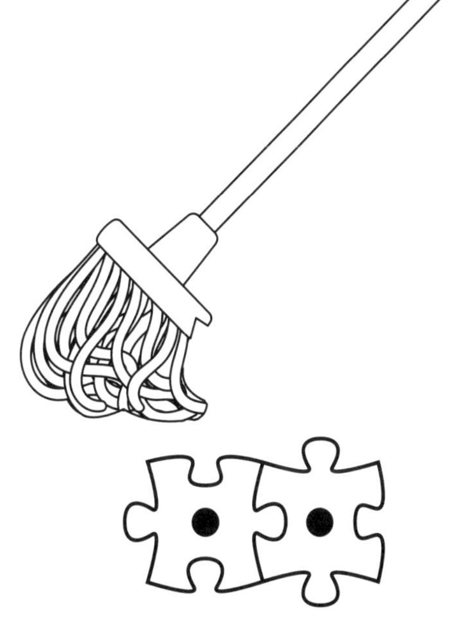

2.

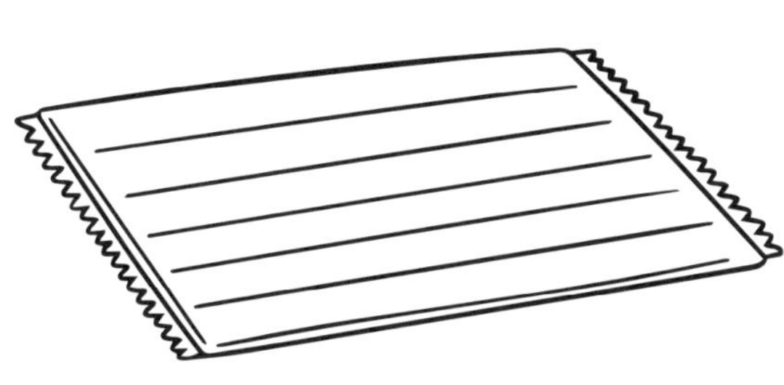

4.

Consonant *Mm*

Directions: Listen as I say the onset and rime for the first picture. *(Say the onset and rime for the first picture: /m/ /an/)* Next, touch the dot in each puzzle piece as I repeat the onset and rime in the word. *(Repeat the onset and rime /m/ /an/.)* Run your finger across the puzzle pieces as we say the onset and rime together. What word is this? *(Repeat this process for all the pictures.)* Then, color the pictures.

Name: ________________________

1.

3.

2.

4.

Directions: Listen as I say the word and the onset and rime for the first picture. *(Say the word* mad. *Then, say it slowly, stretching it out into onset and rime: /m/ /ad/.)* Touch the dot in each puzzle piece as you say the onset and rime. Say the word again. This time, color the dots as you say the onset and rime. *(Repeat this process for all the pictures.)* Then, color the pictures.

Name: ______________________

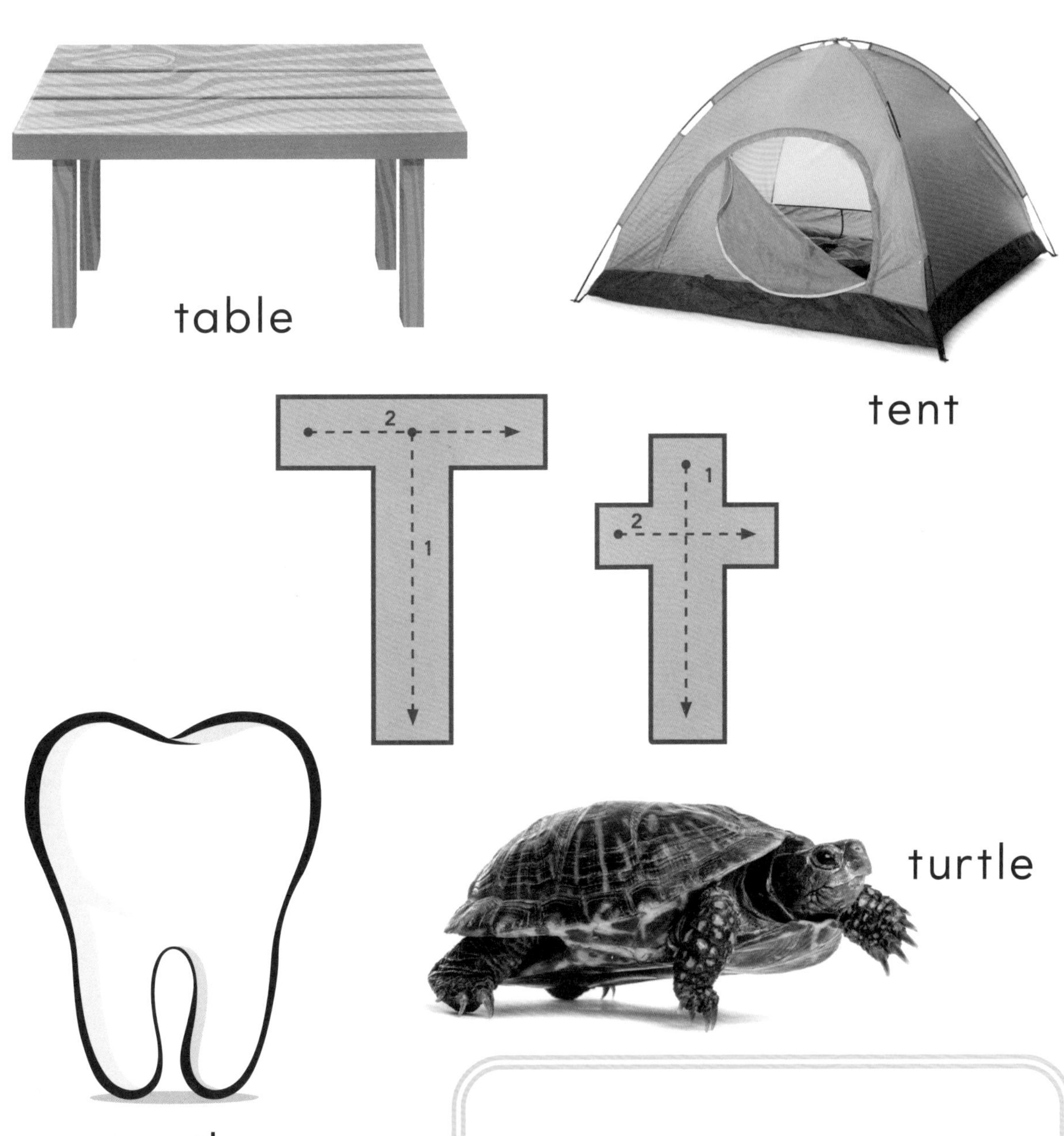

Directions: Trace the letters *T* and *t* with your finger while saying the sound /t/. Repeat this sound while skywriting the letters. Name each picture, listening for the /t/ sound. Find something around you that begins with the /t/ sound. Draw it in the box.

Name: ______________________

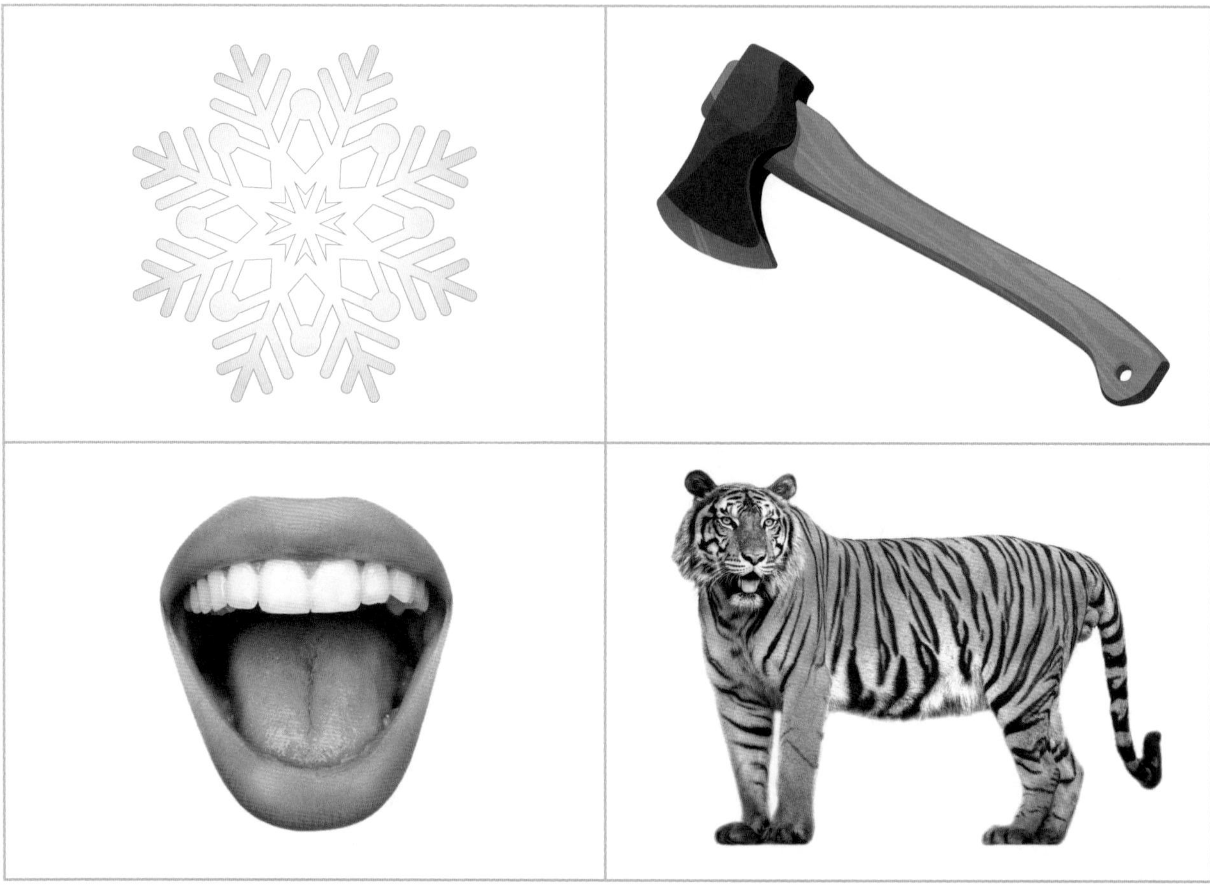

Directions: Name each picture. Say the first sound you hear in each word. Circle the picture that begins with the /t/ sound. Draw an item that begins with the /t/ sound in the box.

Try This!

Use toys to create the letters *T* and *t*. Practice making the /t/ sound each time you form the letters.

Name: ______________________________

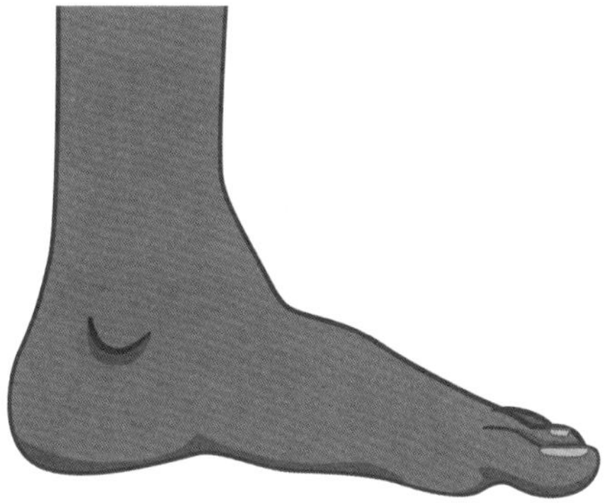

Directions: Name each picture in the table. Say the first sound you hear in each word. Circle the picture that begins with the /t/ sound. Look at the pictures below. Color the images that begin with the /t/ sound.

Name: ________________________

Consonant *Tt*

1.

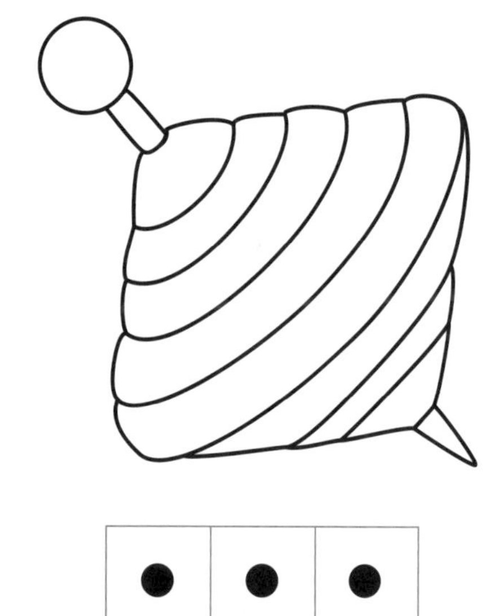

3.

2.

4.

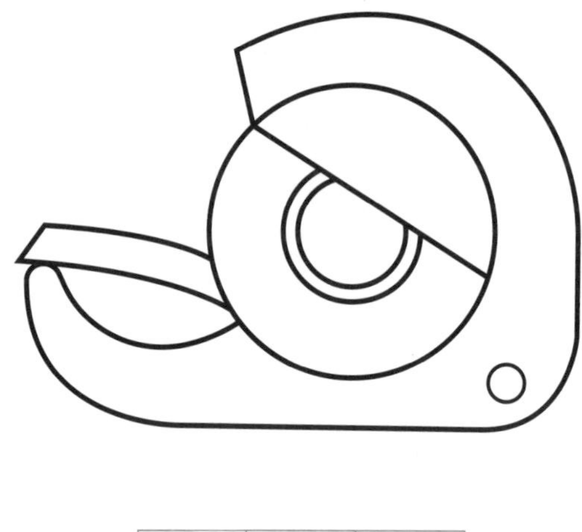

Directions: Listen as I say the sounds for the first picture. *(Say the sounds for the first picture: /t/ /ŏ/ /p/.)* Touch the dot in each box as I repeat each sound in the word. *(Repeat the sounds /t/ /ŏ/ /p/.)* Run your finger across the boxes as we say the sounds together. What word is this? *(Repeat this process for all the pictures.)* Then, color the pictures.

Try This!

Form small balls with clay. Place them in the boxes above. Squish each ball as you say each sound.

Name: ______________________

1.

○ ○ ○

2.

○ ○ ○

3.

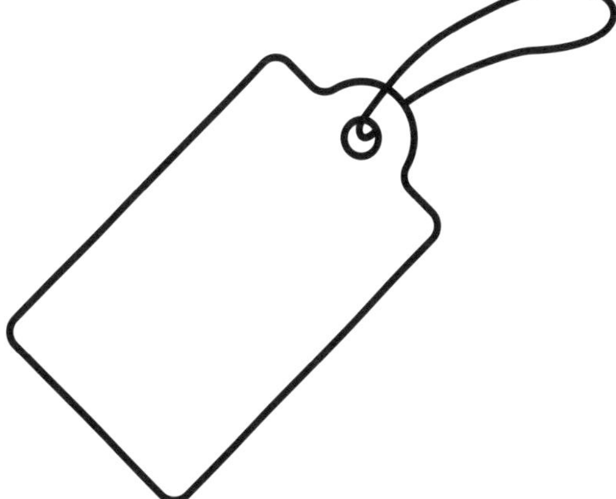

○ ○ ○

4.

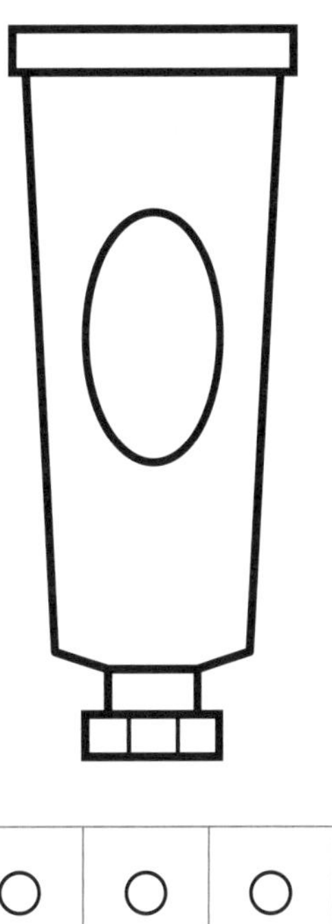

○ ○ ○

Directions: Listen as I say the word and each sound in the word for the first picture. *(Say the word* tug. *Then, say it slowly, stretching out each sound: /t/ /ŭ/ /g/.)* Touch the dot in each box as you say each sound in the word. Say the word again. This time, color the dots as you repeat the sounds in the word. *(Repeat this process for all the pictures.)* Then, color the pictures.

Name: ____________________

Directions: Trace the letters *S* and *s* with your finger while saying the sound /s/. Repeat this sound while skywriting the letters. Name each picture, listening for the /s/ sound. Find something around you that begins with the /s/ sound. Draw it in the box.

Name: ______________________

Try This!

Make a letter *S* collage. Cut out Ss of different sizes. Practice making the /s/ sound as you glue each letter onto construction paper.

Directions: Name each picture. Say the first sound you hear in each word. Circle the picture that begins with the /s/ sound. Draw an item that begins with the /s/ sound in the box.

Name: ______________________

Directions: Name each picture in the table. Say the first sound you hear in each word. Circle the picture that begins with the /s/ sound. Look at the pictures below. Color the images that begin with the /s/ sound.

Name: ______________________

Consonant Ss

1.

3.

2.

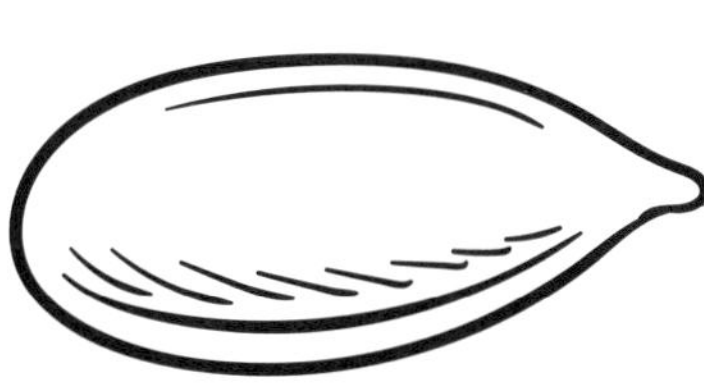

4.

Directions: Listen as I say the onset and rime for the first picture. *(Say the onset and rime for the first picture: /s/ /it/.)* Touch the dot in each puzzle piece as I repeat the onset and rime in the word. *(Repeat the onset and rime /s/ /it/.)* Run your finger across the puzzle pieces as we say the onset and rime together. What word is this? *(Repeat this process for all the pictures.)* Then, color the pictures.

Name: ______________________

Consonant *Ss*

1.

2.

3.

4.

Directions: Listen as I say the word and the onset and rime for the first picture. *(Say the word* sun. *Then, say it slowly, stretching it out into onset and rime: /s/ /un/.)* Touch the dot in each puzzle piece as you say the onset and rime. Say the word again. This time, color the dots as you repeat the onset and rime. *(Repeat this process for all the pictures.)* Then, color the pictures.

Name: ______________________

Directions: Trace the letters *P* and *p* with your finger while saying the sound /p/. Repeat this sound while skywriting the letters. Name each picture, listening for the /p/ sound. Find something around you that begins with the /p/ sound. Draw it in the box.

Name: ______________________

Directions: Name each picture. Say the first sound you hear in each word. Circle the picture that begins with the /p/ sound. Draw an item that begins with the /p/ sound in the box.

Try This!

Use dried pasta to build the letters *P* and *p*. Make the /p/ sound each time you add a piece.

Name: ______________________________

Directions: Name each picture in the table. Say the first sound you hear in each word. Circle the picture that begins with the /p/ sound. Look at the pictures below. Color the images that begin with the /p/ sound.

Name: ______________________

Consonant *Pp*

1.

● ● ●

3.

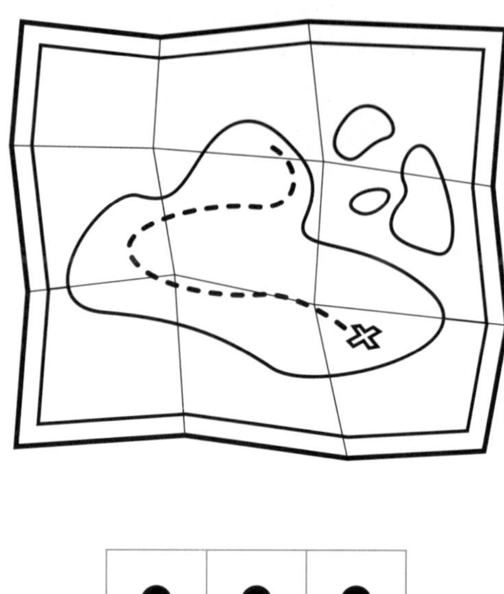

● ● ●

2.

● ● ●

4.

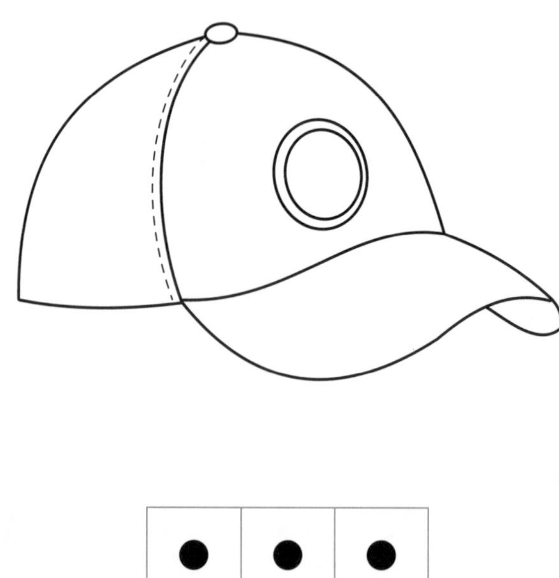

● ● ●

Directions: Listen as I say the sounds for the first picture. *(Say the sounds for the first picture: /p/ /ĭ/ /g/.)* Touch the dot in each box as I repeat each sound in the word. *(Repeat the sounds /p/ /ĭ/ /g/.)* Run your finger across the boxes as we say the sounds together. What word is this? *(Repeat this process for all the pictures.)* Then, color the pictures.

Name: ______________________

1.

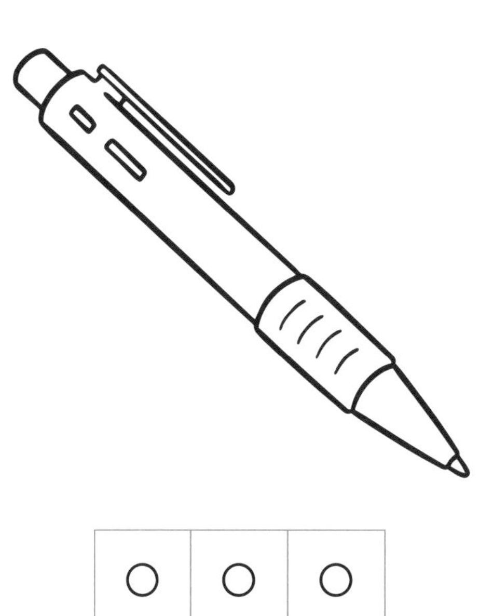

○ ○ ○

3.

○ ○ ○

2.

○ ○ ○

4.

○ ○ ○

Consonant *Pp*

Directions: Listen as I say the word and each sound in the word for the first picture. *(Say the word* pen. *Then, say it slowly, stretching out each sound: /p/ /ĕ/ /n/.)* Touch the dot in each box as you say each sound in the word. Say the word again. This time, color the dots as you repeat the sounds in each word. *(Repeat this process for all the pictures.)* Then, color the pictures.

Name: ______________________

astronaut

alligator

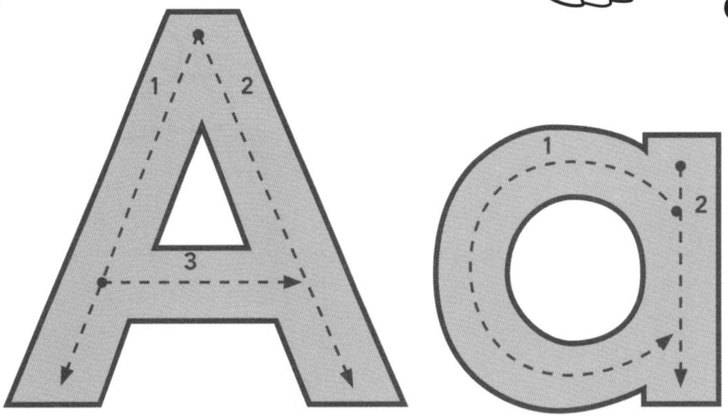

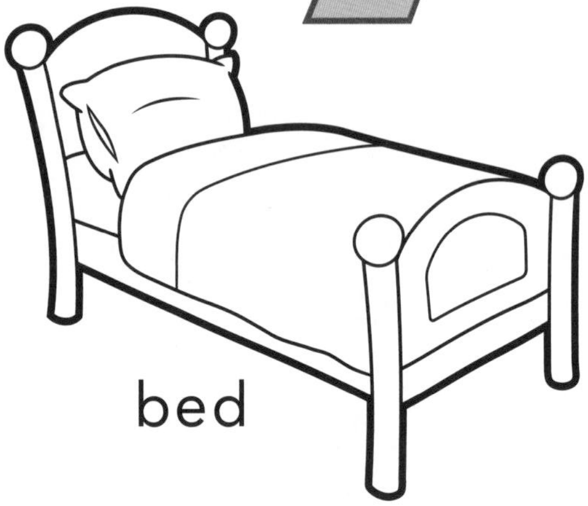

Aa

apple

bed

nest

Directions: Trace the letters *A* and *a* with your finger while saying the sound /ă/. Name each picture. Say the first sound you hear in each word. Color the pictures that begin with the /ă/ sound. Write an *X* on the pictures that do not.

Try This!

Go on a letter hunt. Look for the letters *a*, *m*, *t*, *s*, and *p*. When you find them, skywrite them while you say their sounds.

Name: ______________________

Directions: Trace the letters *M* and *m* with your finger while saying the sound /m/. Name each picture. Say the first sound you hear in each word. Color the pictures that begin with the /m/ sound. Draw a line connecting each picture that begins with /m/ to the letters *M* and *m*.

Name: ____________________

Directions: Trace the letters *T* and *t* with your finger while saying the sound /t/. Name each picture. Say the first sound you hear in each word. Color the pictures that begin with the /t/ sound. Draw two items that begin with the /t/ sound in the box.

Try This!

Write *a*, *m*, *t*, *s*, and *p* on the ground with chalk. Listen as an adult says words. Throw a bean bag on the letter each word starts with.

Name: ______________________________

2.

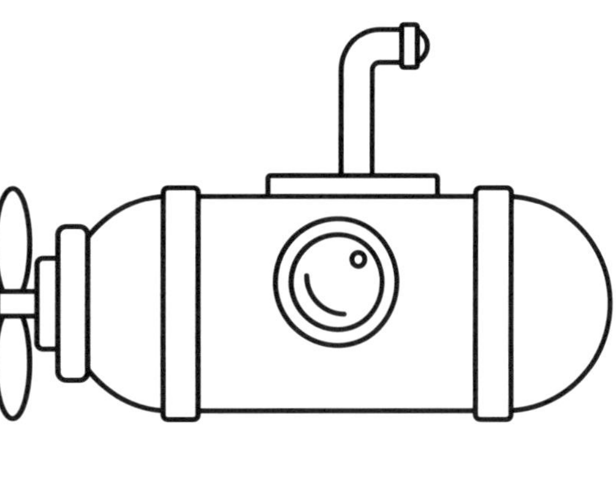

1.

3.

Directions: Trace the letters with your finger while saying the sound /s/. Listen as I say the sounds for the first picture. *(Say the sounds for the first picture: /s/ /ŭ/ /n/.)* Touch the dot in each box as I repeat each sound. *(Repeat the sounds /s/ /ŭ/ /n/.)* Run your finger across the boxes as we say the sounds together. What word is this? *(Repeat this process for all the pictures.)* Then, color the pictures.

Name: ______________________

Pp

2.

○ ○ ○

1.

○ ○ ○

3.

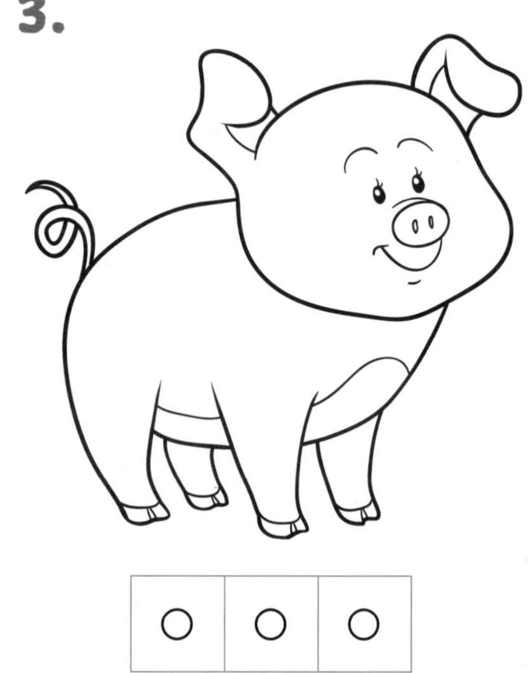

○ ○ ○

Directions: Trace the letters *P* and *p* with your finger while saying the sound /p/. Listen as I say the word and each sound in the word for the first picture. *(Say the word* pup. *Then, say it slowly, stretching out each sound: /p/ /ŭ/ /p/.)* Touch the dot in each box as you say each sound in the word. Say the word again. This time, color the dots as you repeat the sounds in each word. *(Repeat this process for all the pictures.)* Then, color the pictures.

Overview

Short Vowel *Ii* and Consonants *Nn*, *Ff*, *Gg*, and *Bb*

Letters are symbols for phonemes (individual sounds). Phonemes are introduced individually. Developing phonemic awareness includes frequent opportunities to see letters, hear the individual sounds, and practice producing the sounds. Connecting phonemes to familiar vocabulary further develops understanding of letter-sound relationships.

In this unit, students will learn to recognize the letters *i*, *n*, *f*, *g*, and *b* and the sounds they make. Activities for the letter *i* will focus on the short sound /ĭ/.

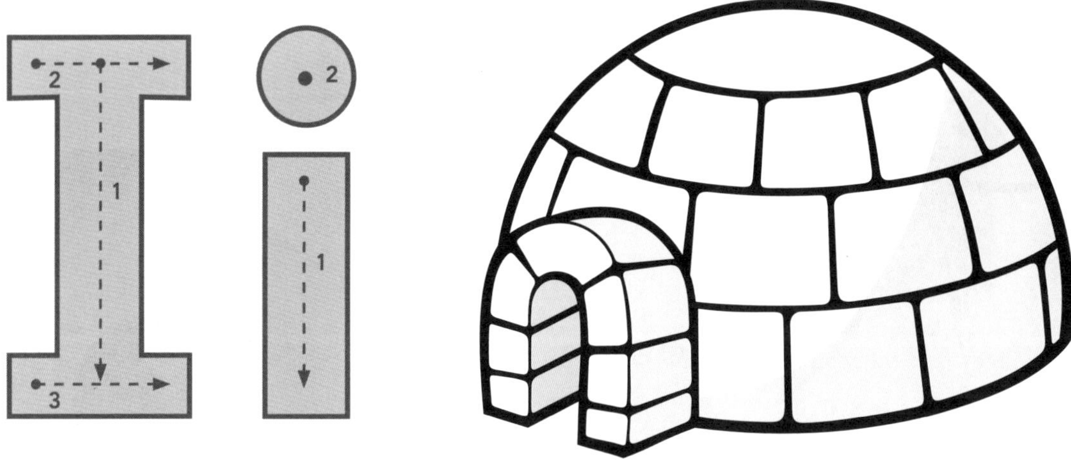

Directions: Look at the letters and picture. In this word, the *i* is pronounced "ih." Trace the letters *I* and *i* with your finger while saying the /ĭ/ sound. Use your finger to skywrite *I* and *i* while making the /ĭ/ sound. *(Name the picture. Ask students to say the first sound they hear in the word.)*

Name: ______________________

iguana

igloo

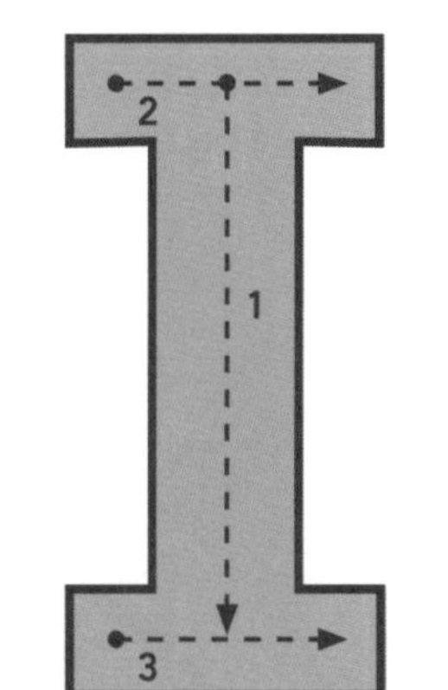

insect

inside

Directions: Trace the letters *I* and *i* with your finger while saying the sound /ĭ/. Repeat this sound while skywriting the letters. Name each picture, listening for the /ĭ/ sound. Find something around you that begins with the /ĭ/ sound. Draw it in the box.

Name: ______________________

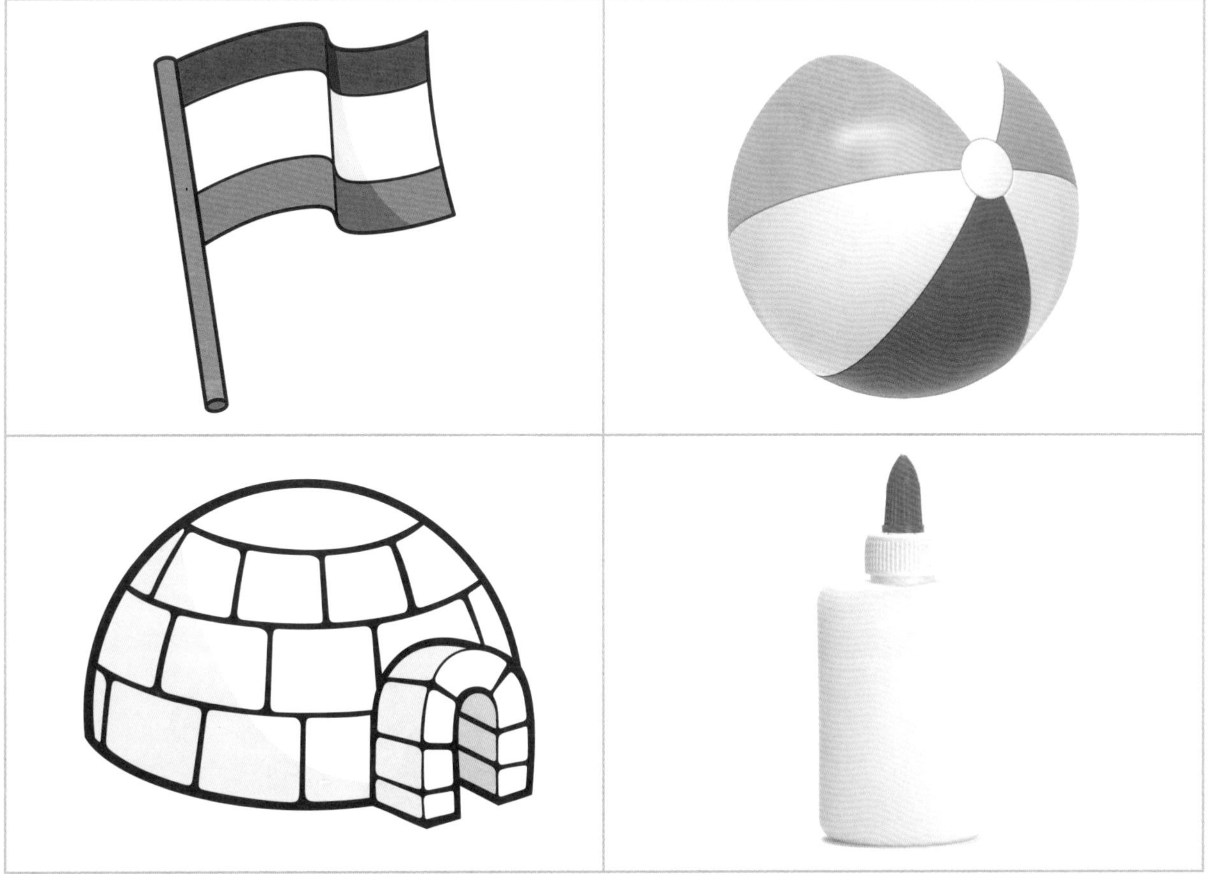

Try This!

Use clay to create items that start with the /ĭ/ sound. Practice making the sound as you sculpt.

Directions: Name each picture. Say the first sound you hear in each word. Circle the picture that begins with the /ĭ/ sound. Draw something that begins with the /ĭ/ sound in the box.

Name: ______________________________

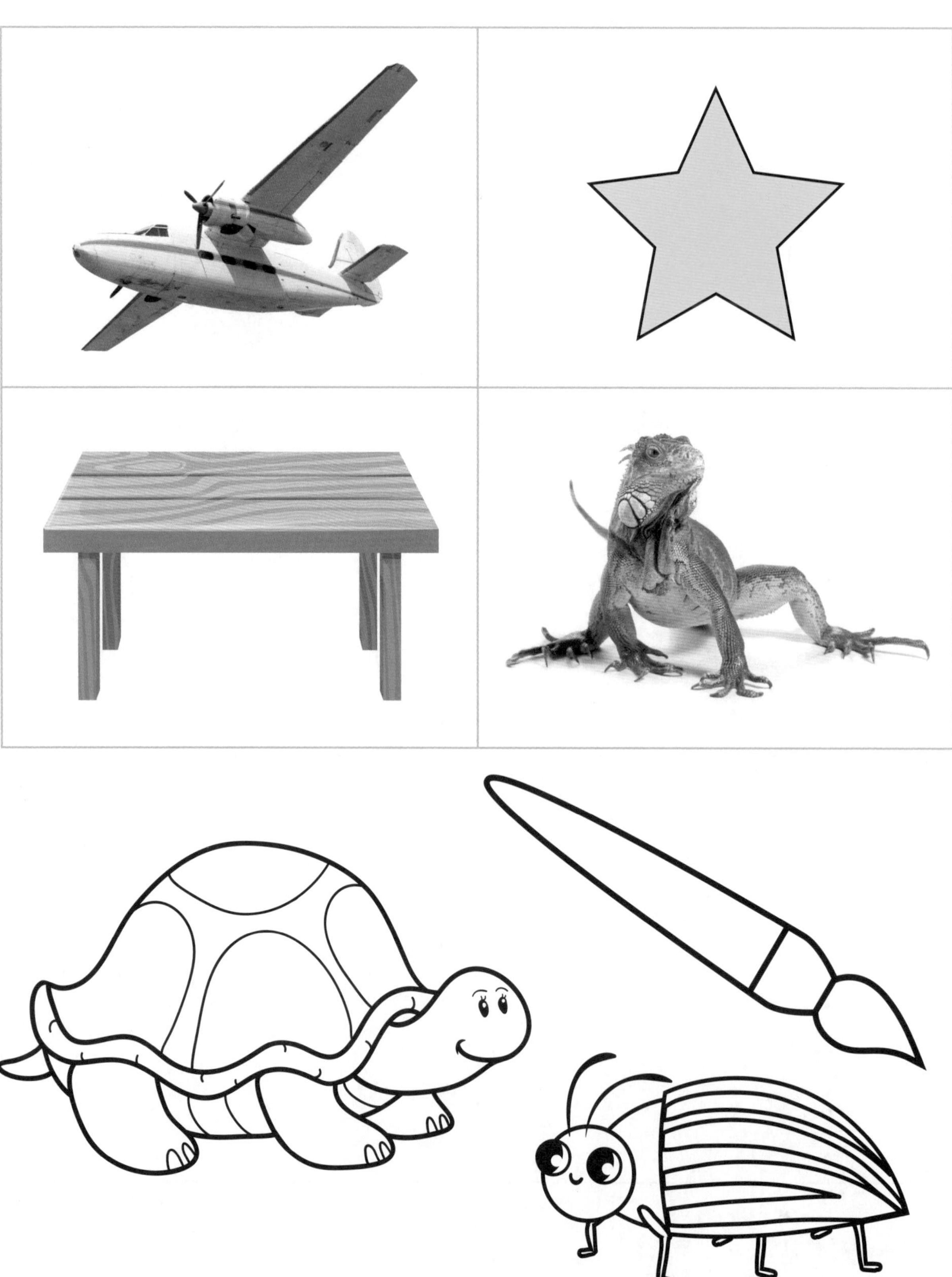

Directions: Name each picture in the table. Say the first sound you hear in each word. Circle the picture that begins with the /ĭ/ sound. Look at the pictures below. Color the image that begins with the /ĭ/ sound.

Name: ______________________

1.

3.

2.

4.

Directions: Listen as I say the syllables for the first picture. *(Say the syllables for the first picture: in-side.)* Touch the dot in each box as I repeat each syllable in the word. *(Repeat the syllables in-side.)* Run your finger across the boxes as we say the sounds together. What word is this? *(Repeat this process for all the pictures:* infant, iguana*, and* instrument.*)* Then, color the pictures.

Name: ____________________

Short *Ii*

1.

3.

2.

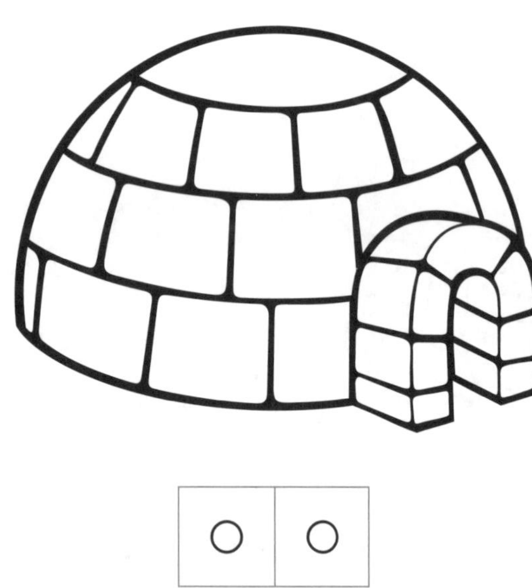

4.

Directions: Listen as I say the word and each syllable in the word for the first picture. *(Say the word* insect *slowly, stretching out each syllable: in-sect.)* Touch the dot in each box as you say each syllable in the word. Say the word again. This time, color the dots as you repeat the sounds in each word. *(Repeat this process for all the pictures:* igloo, into, *and* invitation.*)* Then, color the pictures.

Try This!

Clap your hands as you segment each word into syllables. Count the number of syllables you hear in each word.

Name: ______________________

Consonant *Nn*

Directions: Trace the letters *N* and *n* with your finger while saying the sound /n/. Repeat this sound while skywriting the letters. Name each picture, listening for the /n/ sound. Find something around you that begins with the /n/ sound. Draw it in the box.

Name: ____________________

Consonant *Nn*

Directions: Name each picture. Say the first sound you hear in each word. Circle the picture that begins with the /n/ sound. Draw an item that begins with the /n/ sound in the box.

Try This!

Go on a letter *N* hunt. Each time you find a letter *N* or *n*, trace it with your finger and make the /n/ sound.

Name: ______________________

Directions: Name each picture in the table. Say the first sound you hear in each word. Circle the picture that begins with the /n/ sound. Look at the pictures below. Color the image that begins with the /n/ sound.

Name: ____________________

Consonant *Nn*

1.

3.

2.

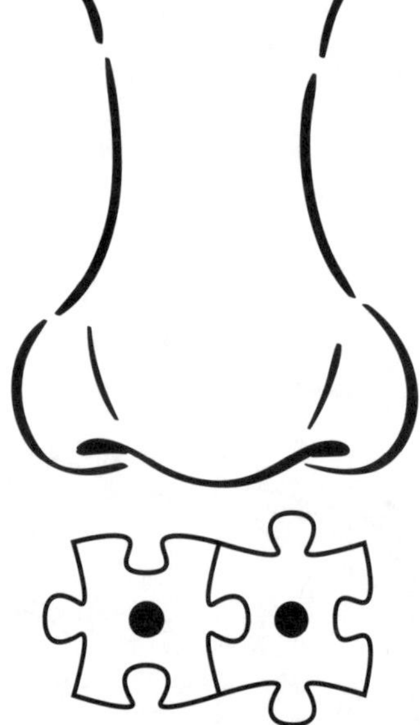

4.

Directions: Listen as I say the onset and rime for the first picture. *(Say the onset and rime for the first picture: /n/ /ut/.)* Touch the dot in each puzzle piece as I repeat the onset and rime in the word. *(Repeat the onset and rime /n/ /ut/.)* Run your finger across the puzzle pieces as we say the onset and rime together. What word is this? *(Repeat this process for all the pictures.)* Then, color the pictures.

Name: ______________________

1.

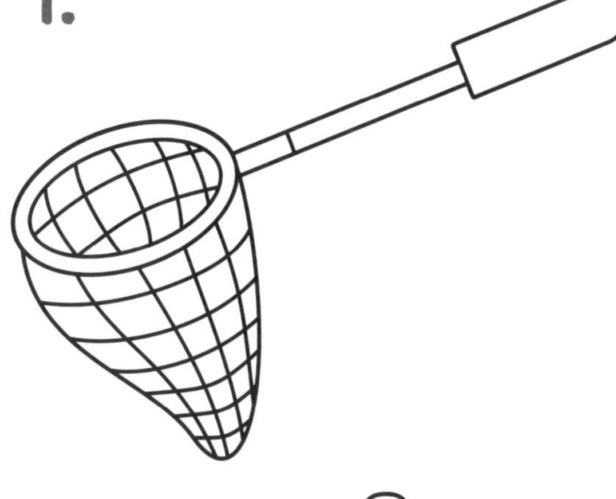

3.

2.

4.

Consonant *Nn*

Try This!

Look for items in nature, such as trees, sticks, and leaves. Segment each object's name into its onset and rime.

Directions: Listen as I say the word and the onset and rime for the first picture. *(Say the word* net. *Then, say it slowly, stretching it out into onset and rime: /n/ /et/.)* Touch the dot in each puzzle piece as you say the onset and rime. Say the word again. This time, color the dots as you repeat the onset and rime. *(Repeat this process for all the pictures:* note, neck, *and* noon.*)* Then, color the pictures.

Name: ____________________

flower

fish

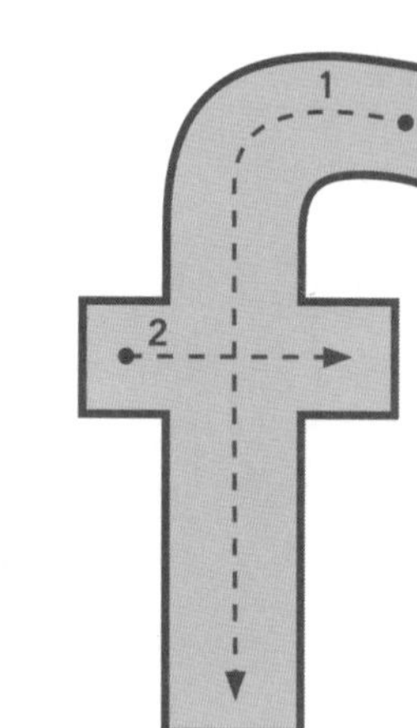

fork

fan

Directions: Trace the letters *F* and *f* with your finger while saying the sound /f/. Repeat this sound while skywriting the letters. Name each picture, listening for the /f/ sound. Find something around you that begins with the /f/ sound. Draw it in the box.

Name: ______________________

Directions: Name each picture. Say the first sound you hear in each word. Circle the picture that begins with the /f/ sound. Draw an item that begins with the /f/ sound in the box.

Name: ____________________

Directions: Name each picture in the table. Say the first sound you hear in each word. Circle the picture that begins with the /f/ sound. Look at the pictures below. Color the images that begin with the /f/ sound.

Try This!

Fill a bag or box with items that start with the /f/ sound. Reach into the bag to feel one of the objects. Try to guess what it is by touch.

Name: ________________________________

1.

3.

2.

4.

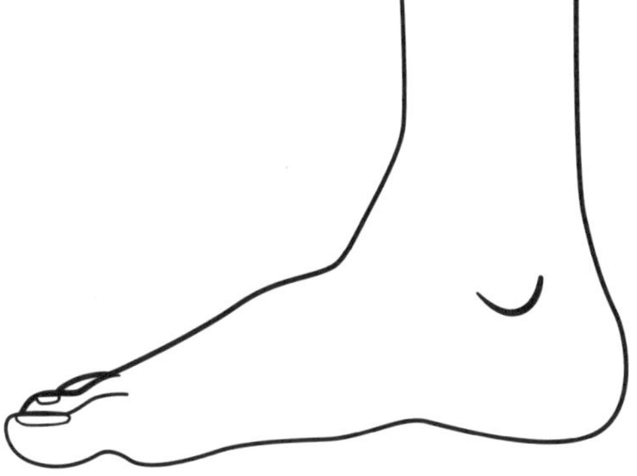

Directions: Listen as I say the sounds for the first picture. *(Say the sounds for the first picture: /f/ /ă/ /n/.)* Touch the dot in each box as I repeat each sound in the word. *(Repeat the sounds /f/ /ă/ /n/.)* Run your finger across the boxes as we say the sounds together. What word is this? *(Repeat this process for all the pictures.)* Then, color the pictures.

Name: ______________________

1.

○	○	○

3.

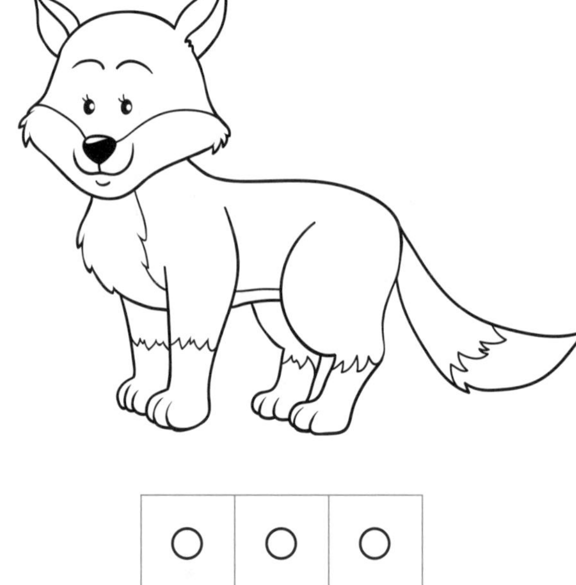

○	○	○

2.

○	○	○

4.

○	○	○	○

Directions: Listen as I say the word and each sound in the word for the first picture. *(Say the word* food. *Then, say it slowly, stretching out each sound: /f/ /oo/ /d/.)* Touch the dot in each box as you say each sound in the word. Say the word again. This time, color the dots as you repeat the sounds in each word. *(Repeat this process for all the pictures.)* Then, color the pictures.

Name: ____________________

garden

gift

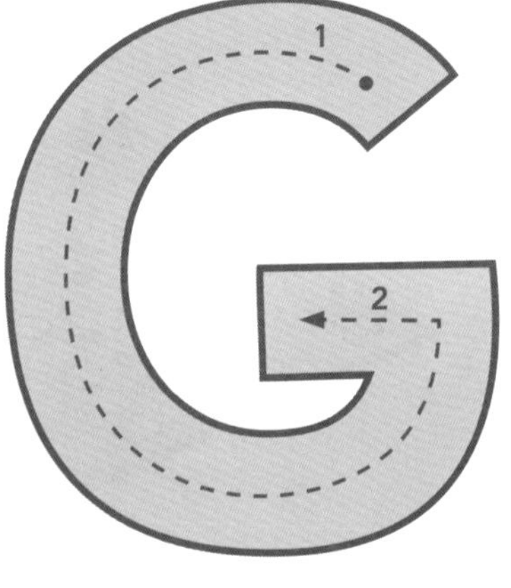

glasses

goat

Directions: Trace the letters *G* and *g* with your finger while saying the sound /g/. Repeat this sound while skywriting the letters. Name each picture, listening for the /g/ sound. Find something around you that begins with the /g/ sound. Draw it in the box.

Name: ______________________

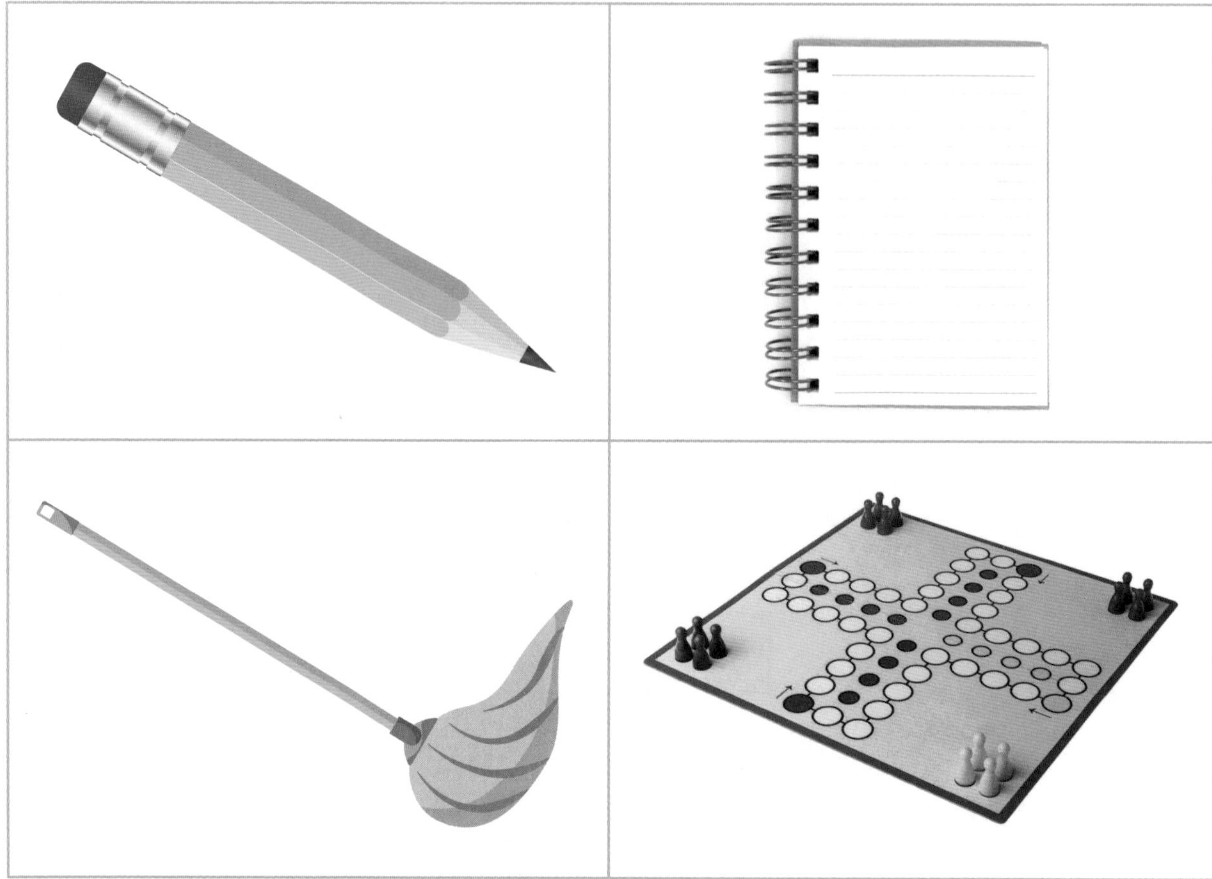

Directions: Name each picture. Say the first sound you hear in each word. Circle the picture that begins with the /g/ sound. Draw an item that begins with the /g/ sound in the box.

Try This!

Place items in a bag. Pull items out of the bag. Name each item, and say its initial sound. Sort the items into two piles: *Starts with /g/* and *Does not start with /g/*.

Name: ____________________

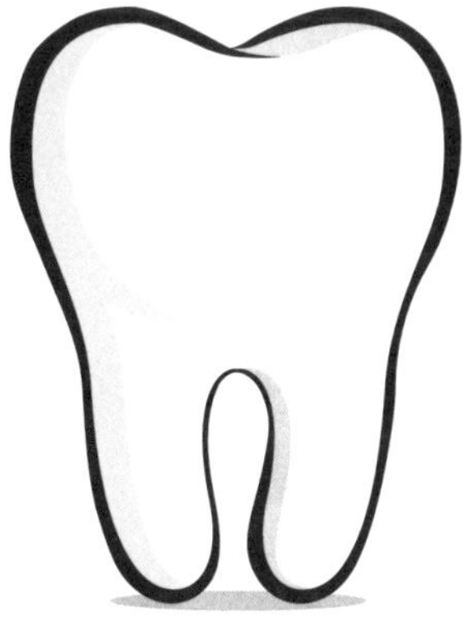

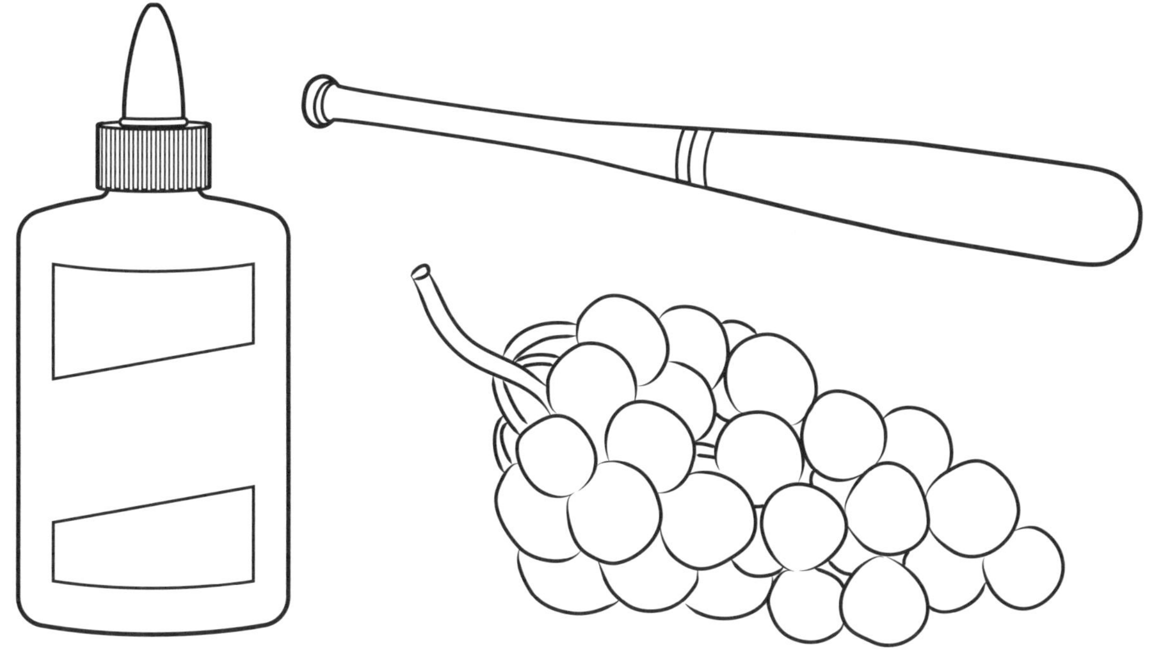

Directions: Name each picture in the table. Say the first sound you hear in each word. Circle the picture that begins with the /g/ sound. Look at the pictures below. Color the images that begin with the /g/ sound.

Consonant Gg

Name: ______________________

Consonant *Gg*

1\.

3\.

2\.

4\.

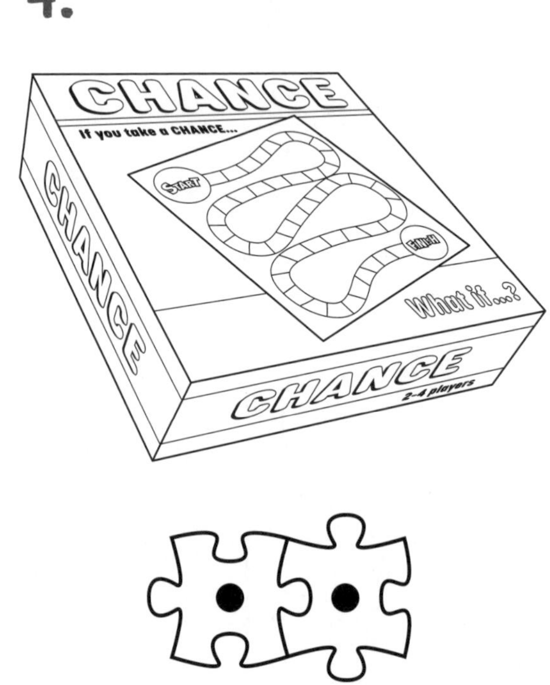

Directions: Listen as I say the onset and rime for the first picture. *(Say the onset and rime for the first picture: /g/ /oat/.)* Touch the dot in each puzzle piece as I repeat the onset and rime in the word. *(Repeat the onset and rime /g/ /oat/.)* Run your finger across the puzzle pieces as we say the onset and rime together. What word is this? *(Repeat this process for all the pictures.)* Then, color the pictures.

Name: ____________________

1.

3.

2.

4.

Try This!

Brainstorm words that start with the /g/ sound. When you think of a word, tap the table or desk to separate the word into onset and rime.

Directions: Listen as I say the word and the onset and rime for the first picture. *(Say the word* ghost. *Then, say it slowly, stretching it out into onset and rime: /gh/ /ost/.)* Touch the dot in each puzzle piece as you say the onset and rime. Say the word again. This time, color the dots as you repeat the onset and rime. *(Repeat this process for all the pictures.)* Then, color the pictures.

Name: ______________________

Directions: Trace the letters *B* and *b* with your finger while saying the sound /b/. Repeat this sound while skywriting the letters. Name each picture, listening for the /b/ sound. Find something around you that begins with the /b/ sound. Draw it in the box.

Name: ______________________

Directions: Name each picture. Say the first sound you hear in each word. Circle the picture that begins with the /b/ sound. Draw an item that begins with the /b/ sound in the box.

Name: ______________________

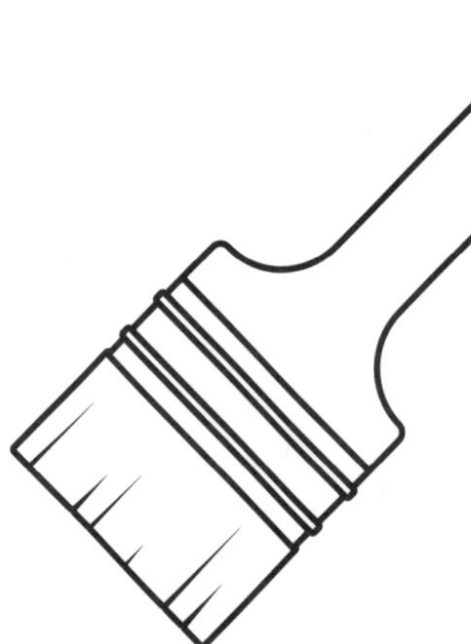

Directions: Name each picture in the table. Say the first sound you hear in each word. Circle the picture that begins with the /b/ sound. Look at the pictures below. Color the images that begin with the /b/ sound.

Try This!

Write or draw a list of activities that start with the /b/ sound. For example, you might like to play basketball, go for a bike ride, or build with blocks.

Name: ______________________

1.

● ● ●

2.

● ● ●

3.

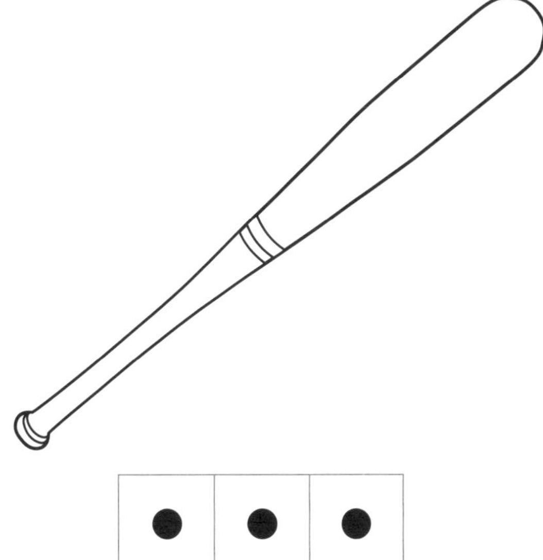

● ● ●

4.

● ● ●

Try This!

Line up three counters or coins under each box. Slide one counter into a box for each sound you hear in the word.

Directions: Listen as I say the sounds for the first picture. *(Say the sounds for the first picture: /b/ /ŭ/ /s/.)* Next, touch the dot in each box as I repeat each sound in the word. *(Repeat the sounds /b/ /ŭ/ /s/.)* Run your finger across the boxes as we say the sounds together. What word is this? *(Repeat this process for all the pictures.)* Then, color the pictures.

Name: ____________________

1.

○ ○ ○

2.

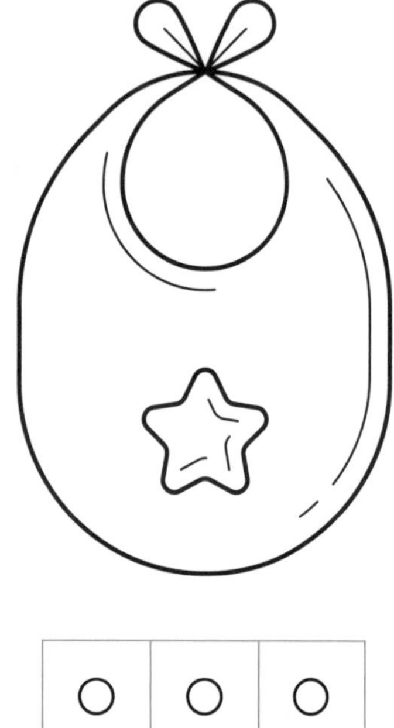

○ ○ ○

3.

○ ○ ○

4.

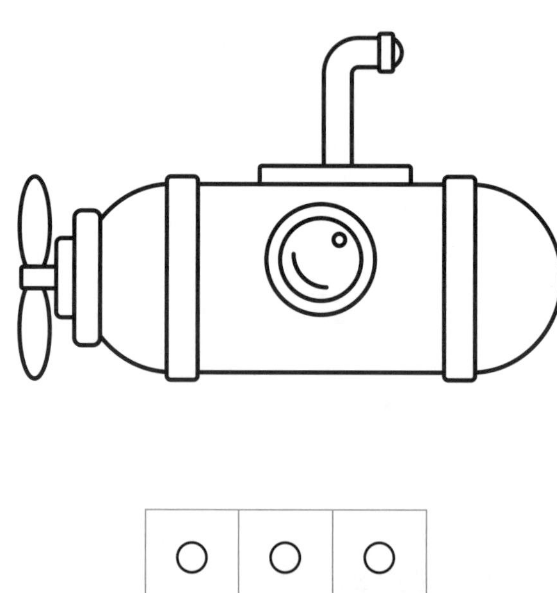

○ ○ ○

Directions: Listen as I say the word and each sound in the word for the first picture. *(Say the word* bed. *Then, say it slowly, stretching out each sound: /b/ /ĕ/ /d/.)* Touch the dot in each box as you say each sound in the word. Say the word again. This time, color the dots as you repeat the sounds in each word. *(Repeat this process for all the pictures.)* Then, color the pictures.

Name: ______________________

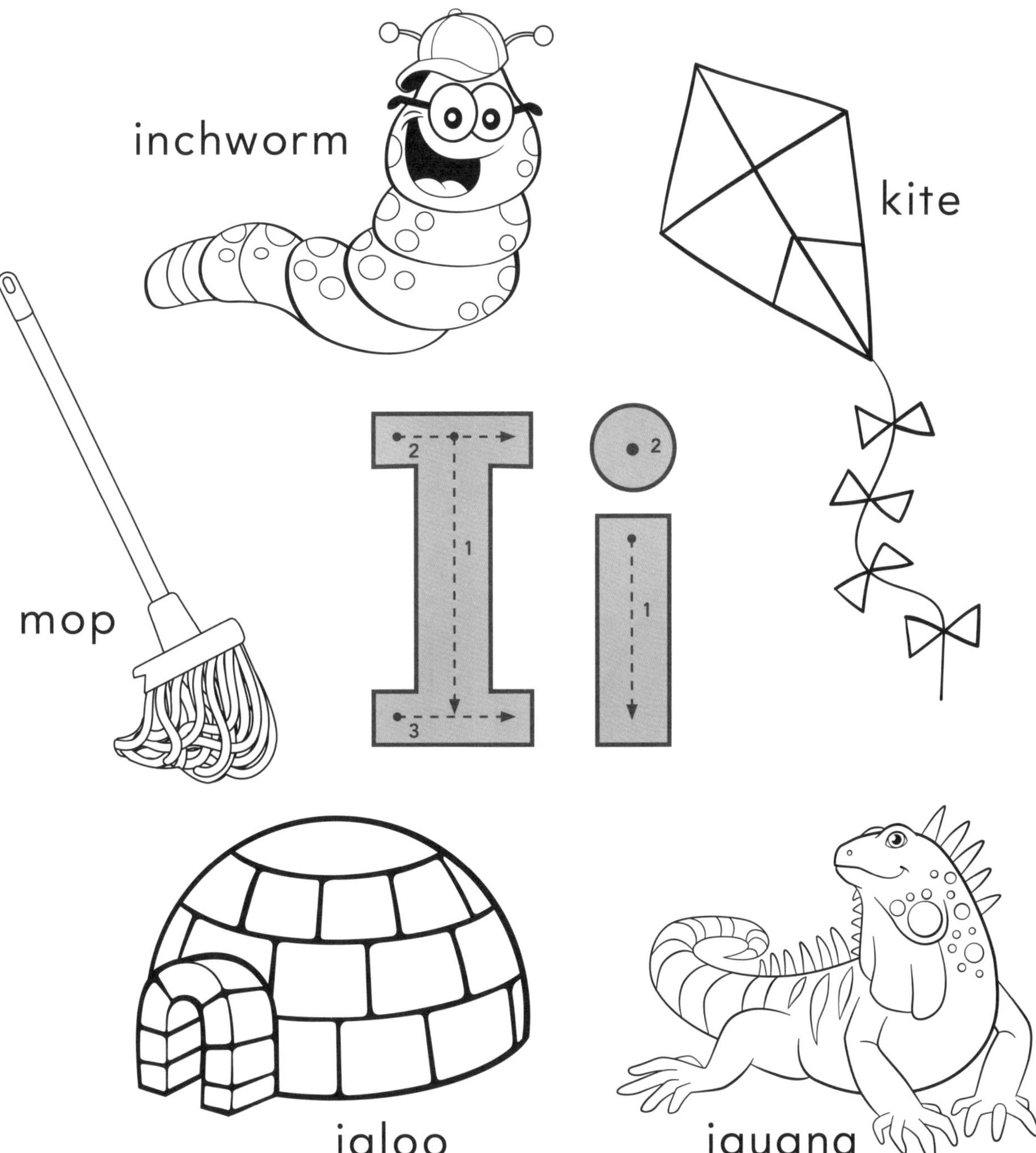

Review: *Ii*, *Nn*, *Ff*, *Gg*, *Bb*

Try This!

Fill a bag or box with items that start with *i*, *n*, *f*, *g*, and *b*. Reach into the bag to feel one of the objects. Try to guess what it is. Once it is guessed correctly, say its initial sound.

Directions: Trace the letters *I* and *i* with your finger while saying the sound /ĭ/. Name each picture. Say the first sound you hear in each word. Color the pictures that begin with the /ĭ/ sound. Write an *X* on the pictures that do not.

Name: ______________________

Directions: Trace the letters *N* and *n* with your finger while saying the sound /n/. Name each picture. Say the first sound you hear in each word. Color the pictures that begin with the /n/ sound. Draw a line connecting each picture that begins with the /n/ sound to the letters *N* and *n*.

Name: ______________________

F f

fan

flower

watch

Try This!

Write *i*, *n*, *f*, *g*, and *b* on note cards. Dance to music until it is paused. Then, the leader will hold up one of the letter cards. Freeze and say the sound for that letter.

Directions: Trace the letters *F* and *f* with your finger while saying the sound /f/. Name each picture. Say the first sound you hear in each word. Color the pictures that begin with the /f/ sound. Draw two items that begin with the /f/ sound in the box.

Name: ______________________

2.

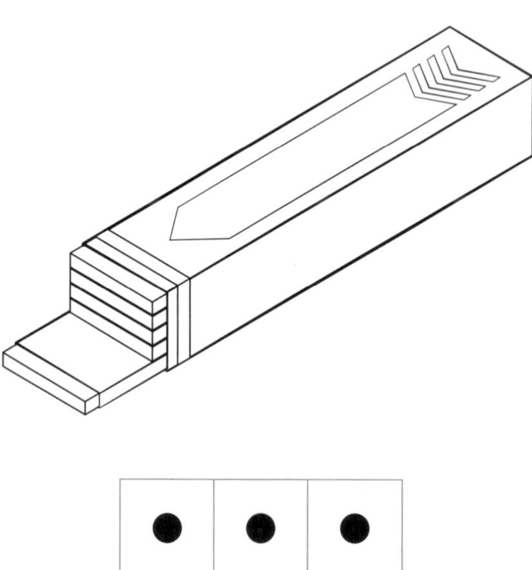

1.

3.

Directions: Trace the letters *G* and *g* with your finger while saying the sound /g/. Listen as I say the sounds for the first picture. *(Say the sounds for the first picture: /g/ /ă/ /p/.)* Touch the dot in each box as I repeat each sound in the word. *(Repeat the sounds /g/ /ă/ /p/.)* Run your finger across the boxes as we say the sounds together. What word is this? *(Repeat this process for all the pictures.)* Then, color the pictures.

Name: ______________________

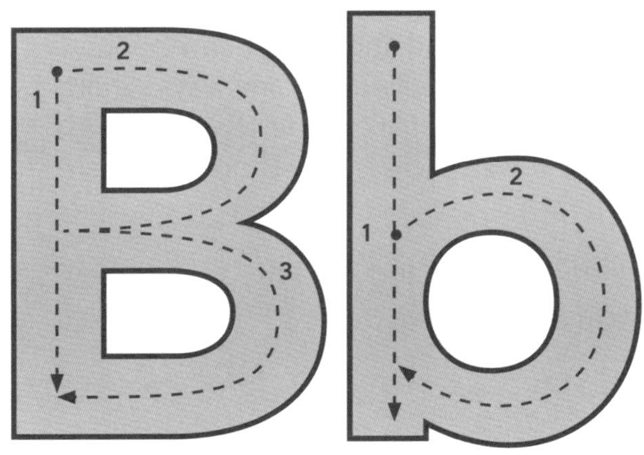

2.

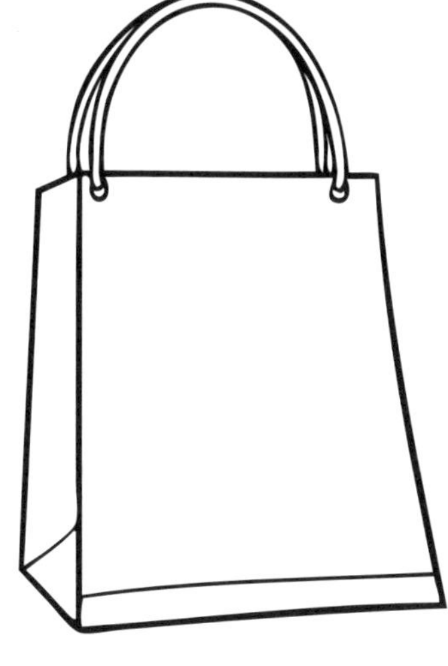

○ ○ ○

1.

○ ○ ○

3.

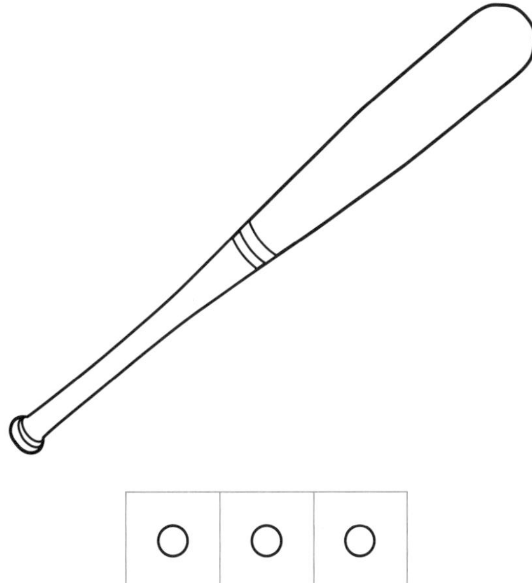

○ ○ ○

Directions: Trace the letters *B* and *b* with your finger while saying the sound /b/. Listen as I say the word and each sound in the word for the first picture. *(Say the word* bun. *Then, say it slowly, stretching out each sound: /b/ /ŭ/ /n/.)* Touch the dot in each box as you say each sound in the word. Say the word again. This time, color the dots as you repeat the sounds in each word. *(Repeat this process for all the pictures.)* Then, color the pictures.

Overview

Short Vowel *Oo* and Consonants *Cc*, *Ll*, *Hh*, and *Jj*

Each vowel can make two different sounds: a long vowel sound and a short vowel sound. Long vowels sound the same as the letter name and can be spelled in many ways. Short vowel sounds are spelled with just the vowel and do not sound like the letter name. All CVC (consonant-vowel-consonant) words have short vowels. This is why short vowels are often taught first.

In this unit, students will learn to recognize the letters *o*, *c*, *l*, *h*, and *j* and the sounds they make. Activities for the letter *o* will focus on the short sound /ŏ/.

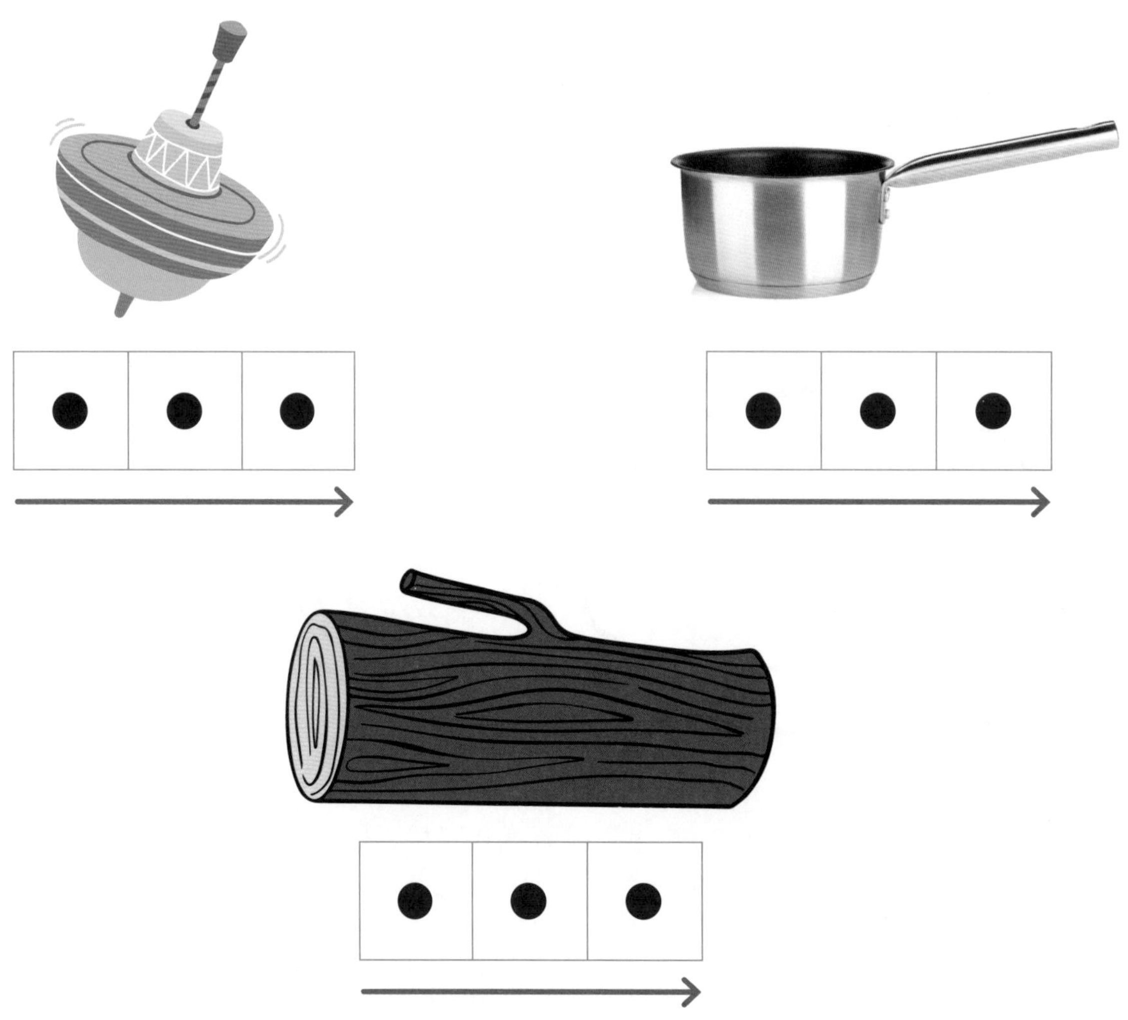

Directions: Look at the pictures. In these words, the *o* is pronounced "awe." Listen for each sound in the word. *(Slowly say the sounds for the first picture, /t/ /ŏ/ /p/, touching one dot for each sound. Then, say the word naturally.)* Touch each dot while I say the sounds again: /t/ /ŏ/ /p/. What sounds did you hear? *(Repeat this process for* pot *and* log.*)*

Name: ____________________

ox

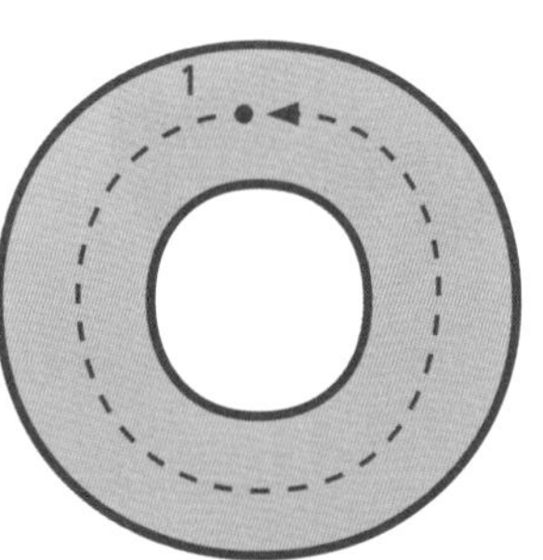

octopus

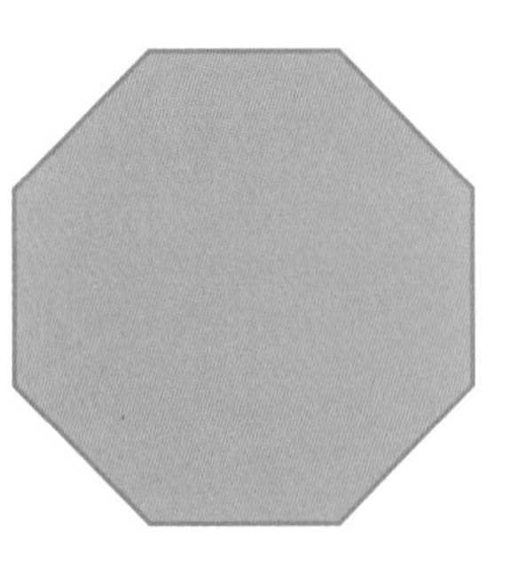

octagon

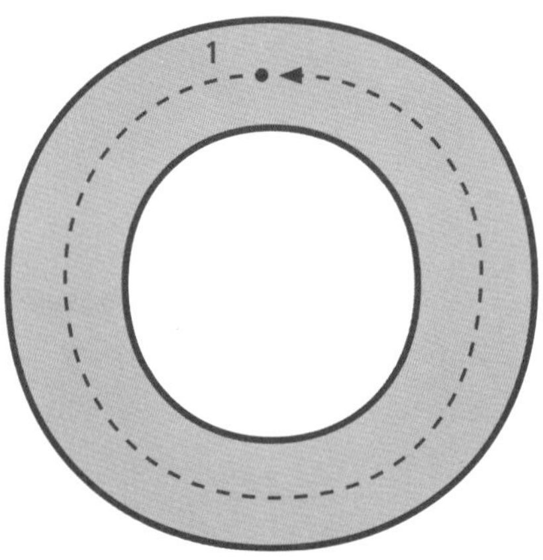

otter

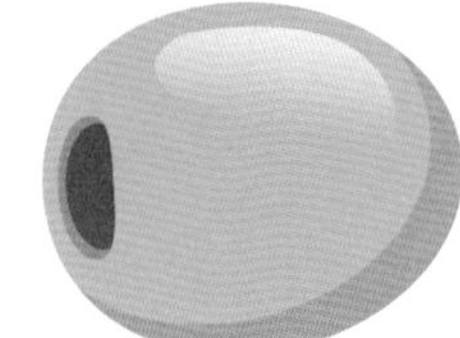

olive

Directions: Trace the letters *O* and *o* with your finger while saying the sound /ŏ/. Repeat this sound while skywriting the letters. Name each picture, listening for the /ŏ/ sound. Find something around you that begins with the /ŏ/ sound. Draw it in the box.

Name: ____________________

Directions: Name each picture. Say the first sound you hear in each word. Circle the picture that begins with the /ŏ/ sound. Draw an item that begins with the /ŏ/ sound in the box.

Try This!

Sprinkle salt, flour, or oatmeal onto a cookie sheet. Practice writing the letters *O* and *o* with your finger or a craft stick. Say the letter sound each time you write it.

Name: ______________________

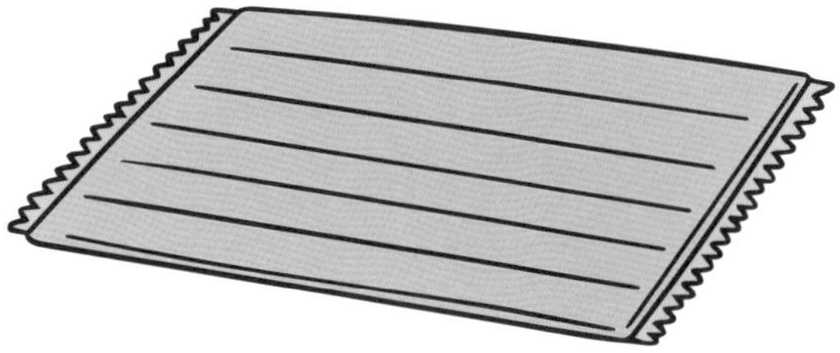

Directions: Name each picture in the table. Say the first sound you hear in each word. Circle the picture that begins with the /ŏ/ sound. Look at the pictures below. Color the image that begins with the /ŏ/ sound.

Name: ____________________

Short *Oo*

1.

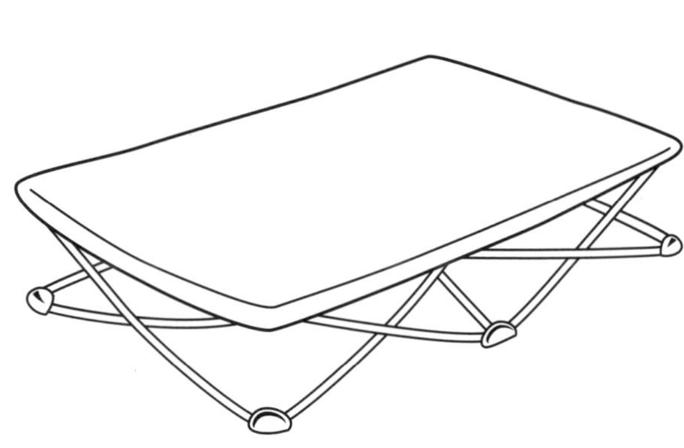

● ● ●

3.

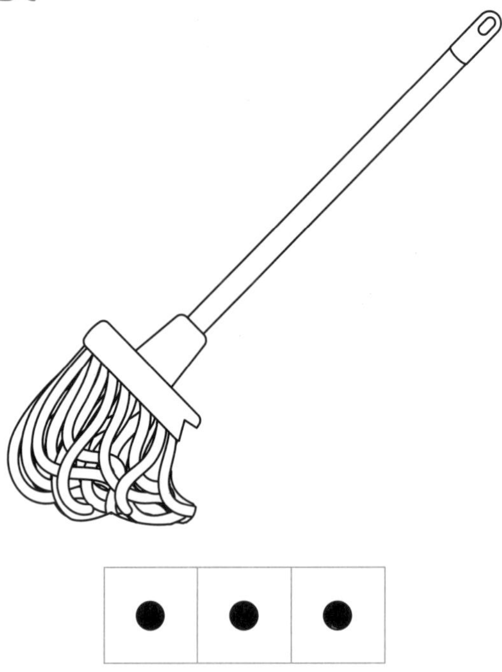

● ● ●

2.

● ● ●

4.

● ● ●

Directions: Listen as I say the sounds for the first picture. *(Say the sounds for the first picture: /c/ /ŏ/ /t/.)* Touch the dot in each box as I repeat each sound in the word. *(Repeat the sounds /c/ /ŏ/ /t/.)* Run your finger across the boxes as we say the sounds together. What word is this? *(Repeat this process for all the pictures.)* Then, color the pictures.

Name: ______________________________

1.

○ ○ ○

3.

○ ○ ○

2.

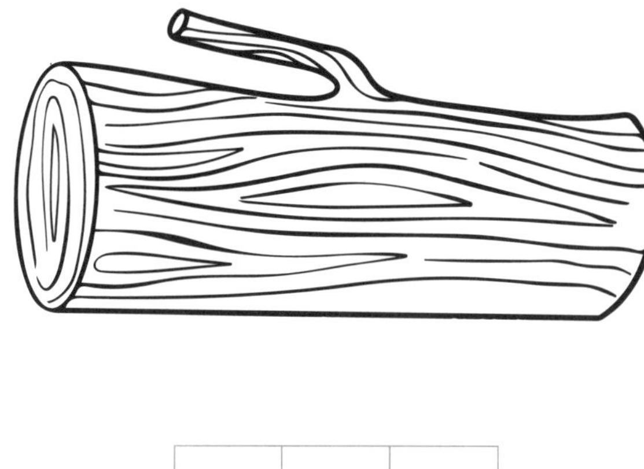

○ ○ ○

4.

○ ○ ○

Short *Oo*

Try This!

Make each sound like a robot as you segment each word above. This will help you clearly hear each phoneme.

Directions: Listen as I say the word and each sound in the word for the first picture. *(Say the word* pot. *Then, say it slowly, stretching out each sound: /p/ /ŏ/ /t/.)* Touch the dot in each box as you say each sound in the word. Say the word again. This time, color the dots as you repeat the sounds in each word. *(Repeat this process for all the pictures.)* Then, color the pictures.

Name: ______________________

cow

cake

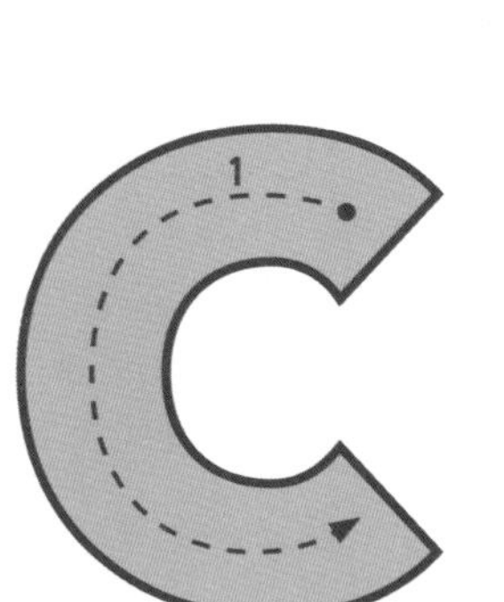

carrot

candle

Directions: Trace the letters *C* and *c* with your finger while saying the sound /c/. Repeat this sound while skywriting the letters. Name each picture, listening for the /c/ sound. Find something around you that begins with the /c/ sound. Draw it in the box.

Name: ______________________

Try This!

Use cotton balls or toy cars to build the letters *C* and *c*. Practice the /c/ sound each time you create it.

Directions: Name each picture. Say the first sound you hear in each word. Circle the picture that begins with the /c/ sound. Draw an item that begins with the /c/ sound in the box.

Name: ____________________

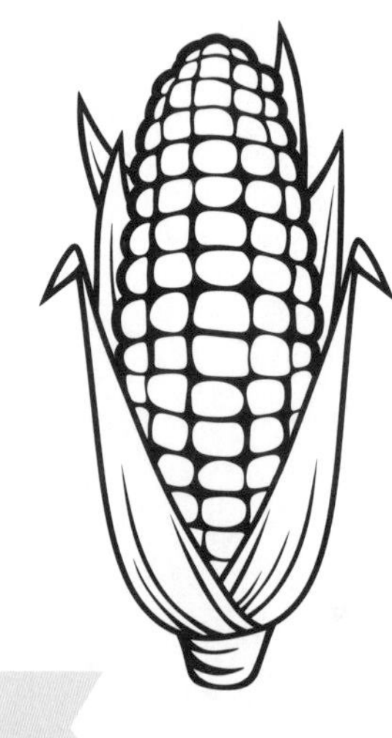

Try This!

Write the letters C and c on at least five sticky notes. Find items around you that start with the /c/ sound. Place a sticky note on each item.

Directions: Name each picture in the table. Say the first sound you hear in each word. Circle the picture that begins with the /c/ sound. Look at the pictures below. Color the images that begin with the /c/ sound.

Name: ______________________

1.

3.

2.

4.

Directions: Listen as I say the onset and rime for the first picture. *(Say the onset and rime for the first picture: /c/ /up/.)* Touch the dot in each puzzle piece as I repeat the onset and rime in the word. *(Repeat the onset and rime /c/ /up/.)* Run your finger across the puzzle pieces as we say the onset and rime together. What word is this? *(Repeat this process for all the pictures.)* Then, color the pictures.

Name: ______________________

Consonant *Cc*

1.

3.

2.

4.

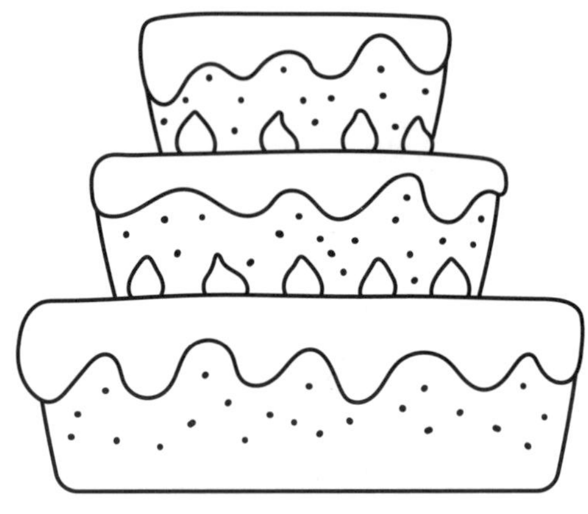

Directions: Listen as I say the word and the onset and rime for the first picture. *(Say the word* car. *Then, say it slowly, stretching it out into onset and rime: /c/ /ar/.)* Touch the dot in each puzzle piece as you say the onset and rime. Say the word again. This time, color the dots as you repeat the onset and rime. *(Repeat this process for all the pictures.)* Then, color the pictures.

Name: ________________________

Consonant *Ll*

Directions: Trace the letters *L* and *l* with your finger while saying the sound /l/. Repeat this sound while skywriting the letters. Name each picture, listening for the /l/ sound. Find something around you that begins with the /l/ sound. Draw it in the box.

Name: ______________________

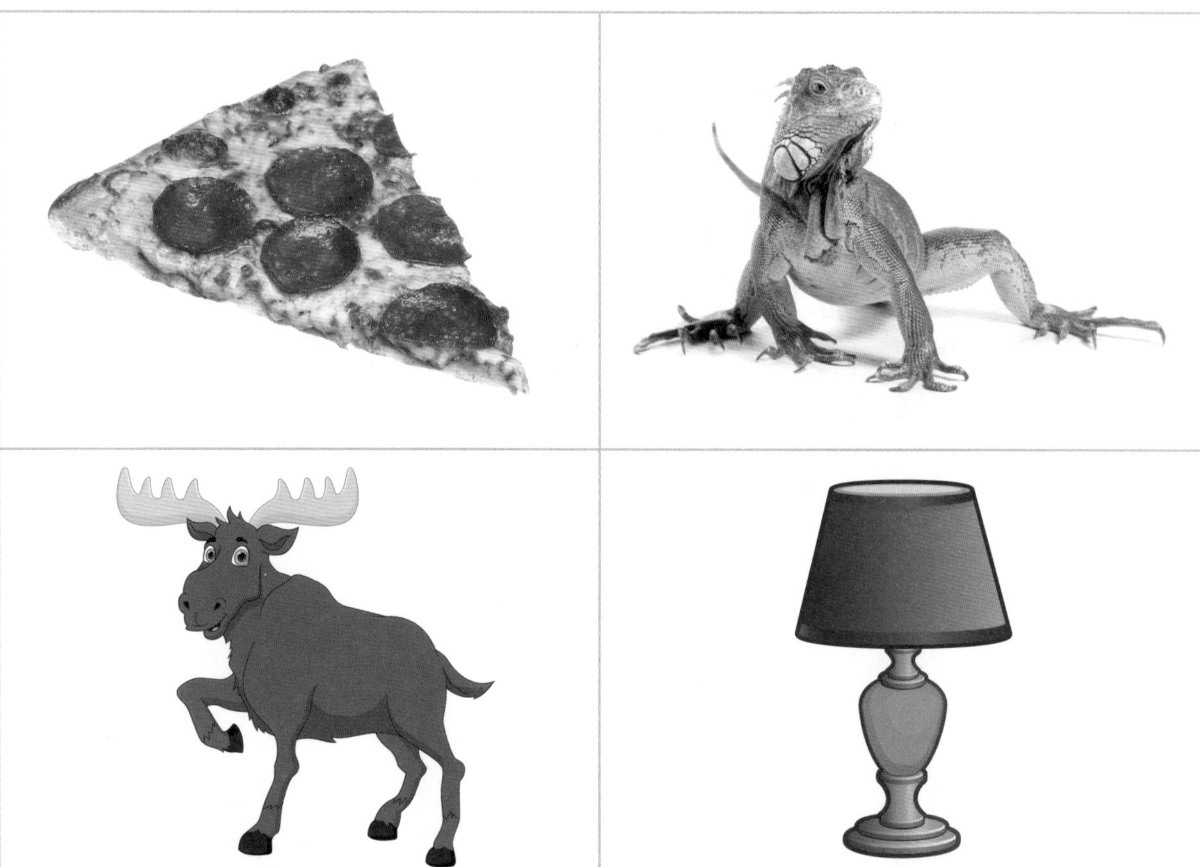

Directions: Name each picture. Say the first sound you hear in each word. Circle the picture that begins with the /l/ sound. Draw an item that begins with the /l/ sound in the box.

Name: ______________________

Directions: Name each picture in the table. Say the first sound you hear in each word. Circle the picture that begins with the /l/ sound. Look at the pictures below. Color the image that begins with the /l/ sound.

Name: ______________________

1.

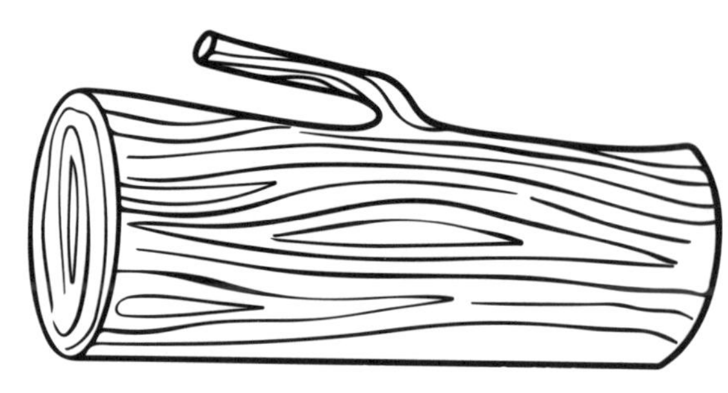

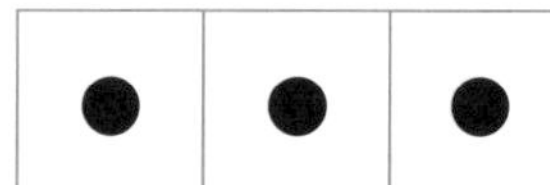

3.

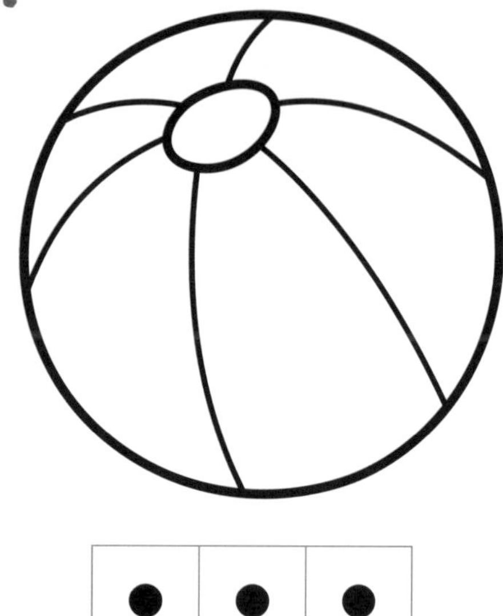

● ● ●

2.

● ● ●

4.

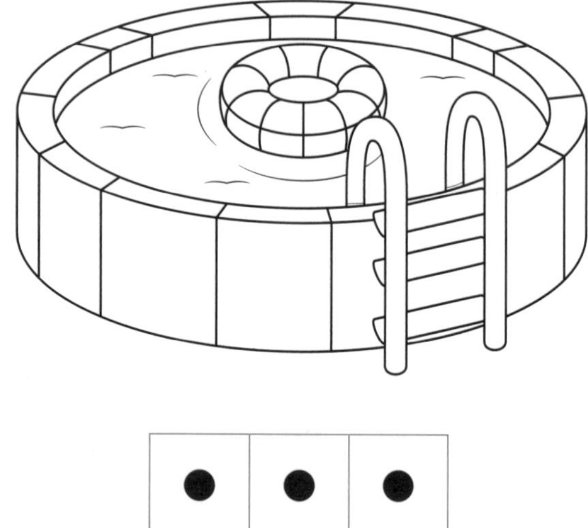

● ● ●

Directions: Listen as I say the sounds for the first picture. *(Say the sounds for the first picture: /l/ /ŏ/ /g/.)* Touch the dot in each box as I repeat each sound in the word. *(Repeat the sounds /l/ /ŏ/ /g/.)* Run your finger across the boxes as we say the sounds together. What word is this? *(Repeat this process for all the pictures.)* Then, color the pictures.

Try This!

Place three beads on one end of a string or pipe cleaner. Slide each bead from one side of the string to the other as you say each sound.

Name: ______________________

1.

○ ○ ○

3.

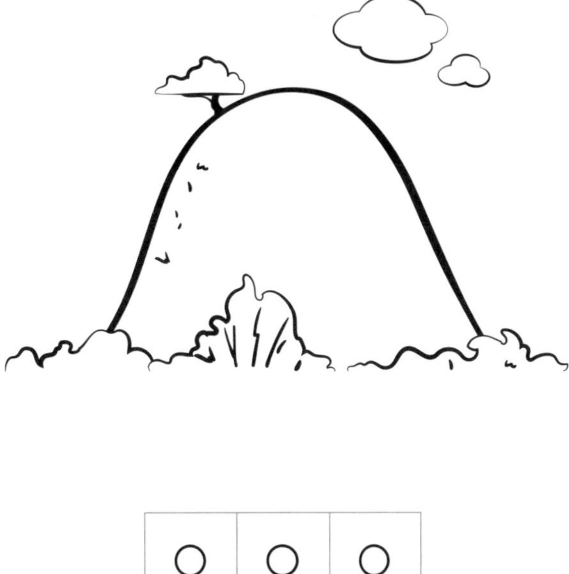

○ ○ ○

2.

○ ○ ○

4.

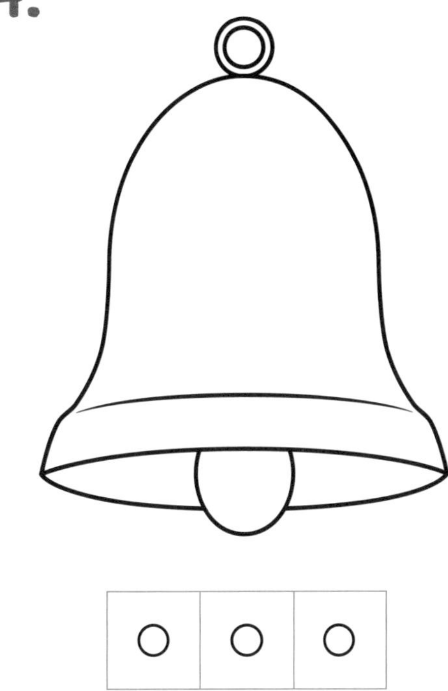

○ ○ ○

Directions: Listen as I say the word and each sound in the word for the first picture. *(Say the word* leg. *Then, say it slowly, stretching out each sound: /l/ /ĕ/ /g/.)* Touch the dot in each box as you say each sound in the word. Say the word again. This time, color the dots as you repeat the sounds in each word. *(Repeat this process for all the pictures.)* Then, color the pictures.

Name: ______________________

hat

horse

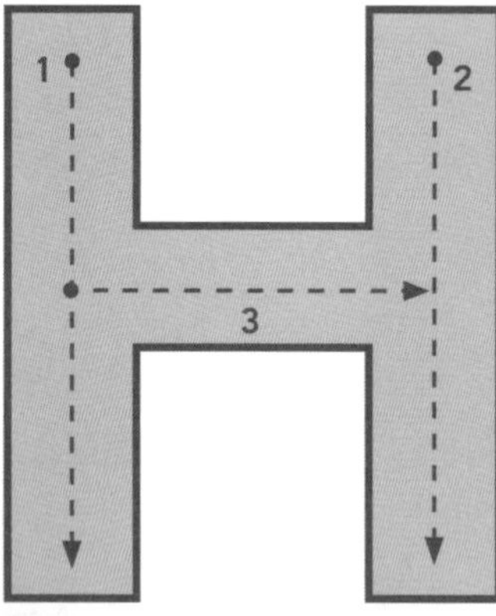
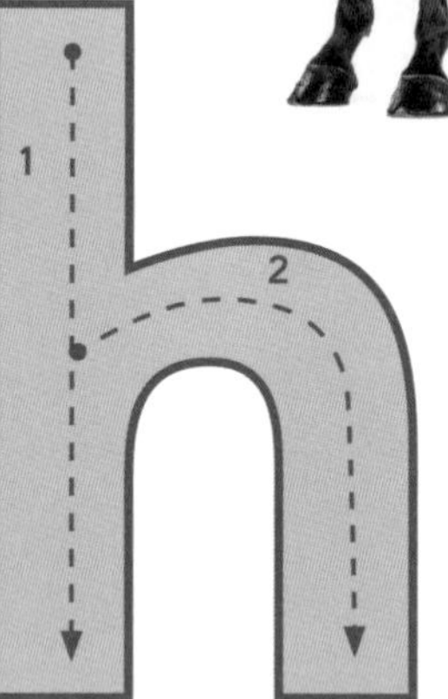

heart

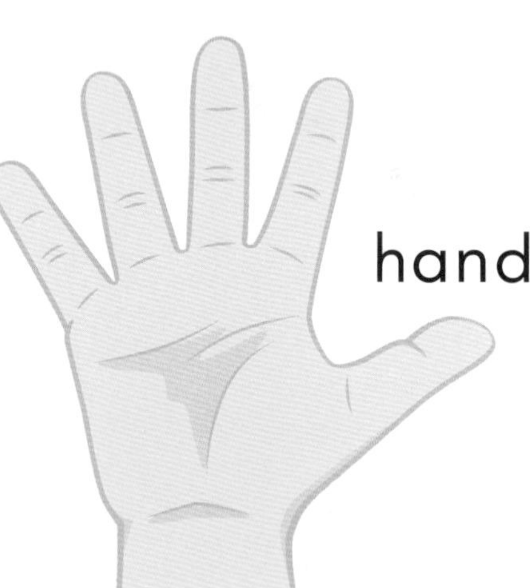

hand

Directions: Trace the letters *H* and *h* with your finger while saying the sound /h/. Repeat this sound while skywriting the letters. Name each picture, listening for the /h/ sound. Find something around you that begins with the /h/ sound. Draw it in the box.

Consonant *Hh*

Name: ______________________

Directions: Name each picture. Say the first sound you hear in each word. Circle the picture that begins with the /h/ sound. Draw an item that begins with the /h/ sound in the box.

Name: ______________________

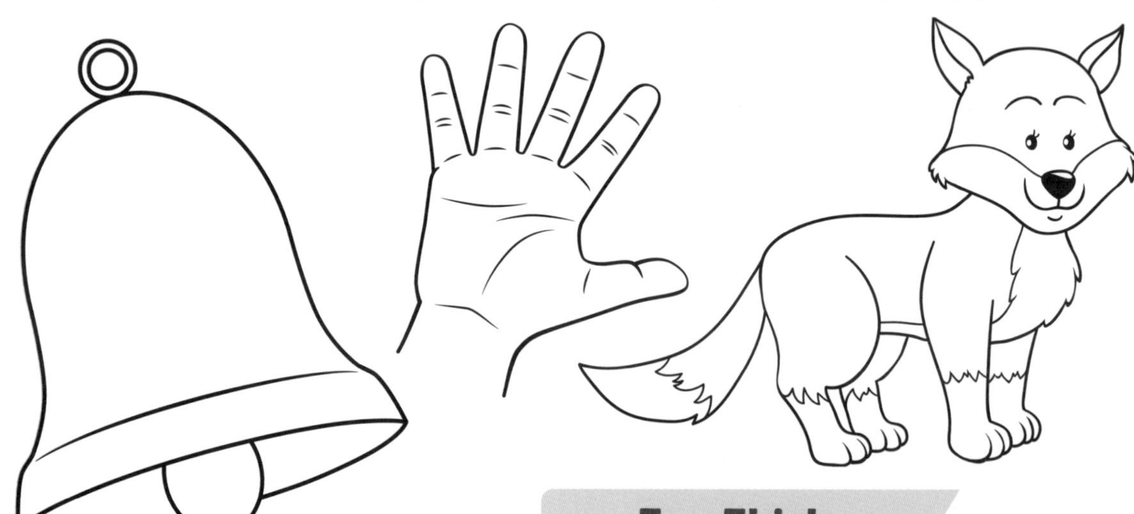

Directions: Name each picture in the table. Say the first sound you hear in each word. Circle the picture that begins with the /h/ sound. Look at the pictures below. Color the image that begins with the /h/ sound.

Try This!

Use a ball to play a letter *H* game. Each player will name one word that starts with the /h/ sound. Then, they pass the ball to the next person.

Name: ______________________

1.

2.

3.

4.

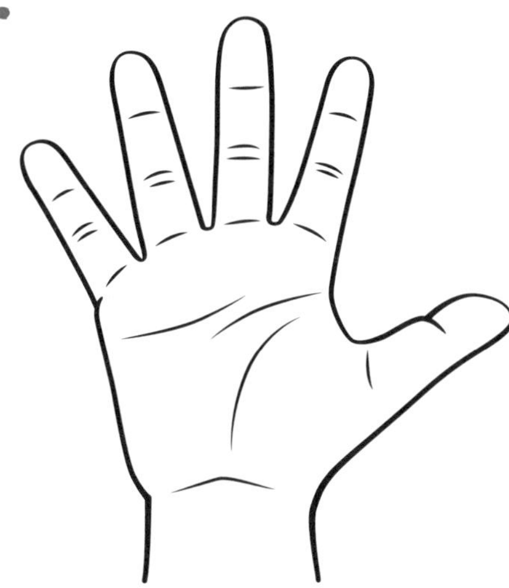

Directions: Listen as I say the sounds for the first picture. *(Say the sounds for the first picture: /h/ /ŏ/ /g/.)* Touch the dot in each box as I repeat each sound in the word. *(Repeat the sounds /h/ /ŏ/ /g/.)* Run your finger across the boxes as we say the sounds together. What word is this? *(Repeat this process for all the pictures.)* Then, color the pictures.

Name: ____________________

Consonant *Hh*

1.

○ ○ ○

3.

○ ○ ○

2.

○ ○ ○

4.

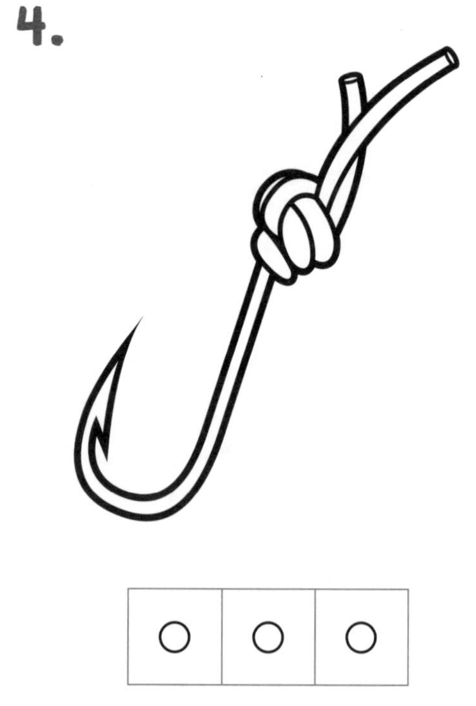

○ ○ ○

Directions: Listen as I say the word and each sound in the word for the first picture. *(Say the word* hen. *Then, say it slowly, stretching out each sound: /h/ /ĕ/ /n/.)* Touch the dot in each box as you say each sound in the word. Say the word again. This time, color the dots as you repeat the sounds in each word. *(Repeat this process for all the pictures.)* Then, color the pictures.

Name: ____________________

Directions: Trace the letters *J* and *j* with your finger while saying the sound /j/. Repeat this sound while skywriting the letters. Name each picture, listening for the /j/ sound. Find something around you that begins with the /j/ sound. Draw it in the box.

Name: ______________________

Directions: Name each picture. Say the first sound you hear in each word. Circle the picture that begins with the /j/ sound. Draw an item that begins with the /j/ sound in the box.

Try This!

Use a paintbrush and water to practice writing the letters *J* and *j* on concrete. Practice making the /j/ sound each time your form the letter.

Name: ______________________

Directions: Name each picture in the table. Say the first sound you hear in each word. Circle the picture that begins with the /j/ sound. Look at the pictures below. Color the image that begins with the /j/ sound.

Name: ______________________

1.

● ● ●

3.

● ● ●

2.

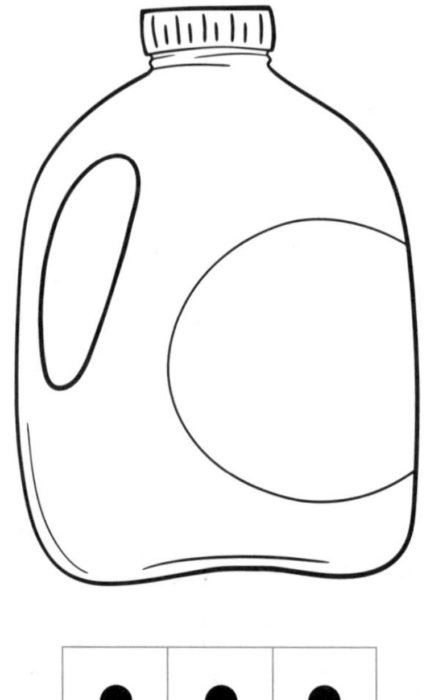

● ● ●

4.

● ● ● ●

Directions: Listen as I say the sounds for the first picture. *(Say the sounds for the first picture: /j/ /ĕ/ /t/.)* Touch the dot in each box as I repeat each sound in the word. *(Repeat the sounds /j/ /ĕ/ /t/.)* Run your finger across the boxes as we say the sounds together. What word is this? *(Repeat this process for all the pictures.)* Then, color the pictures.

Name: ______________________________

1.

3.

2.

4.

Try This!

Use a toy hammer as you segment each word. Tap the hammer onto the table or desk for each sound you hear.

Directions: Listen as I say the word and each sound in the word for the first picture. *(Say the word* June. *Then, say it slowly, stretching out each sound: /j/ /ū/ /n/.)* Touch the dot in each box as you say each sound in the word. Say the word again. This time, color the dots as you repeat the sounds in each word. *(Repeat this process for all the pictures.)* Then, color the pictures.

Name: ______________________

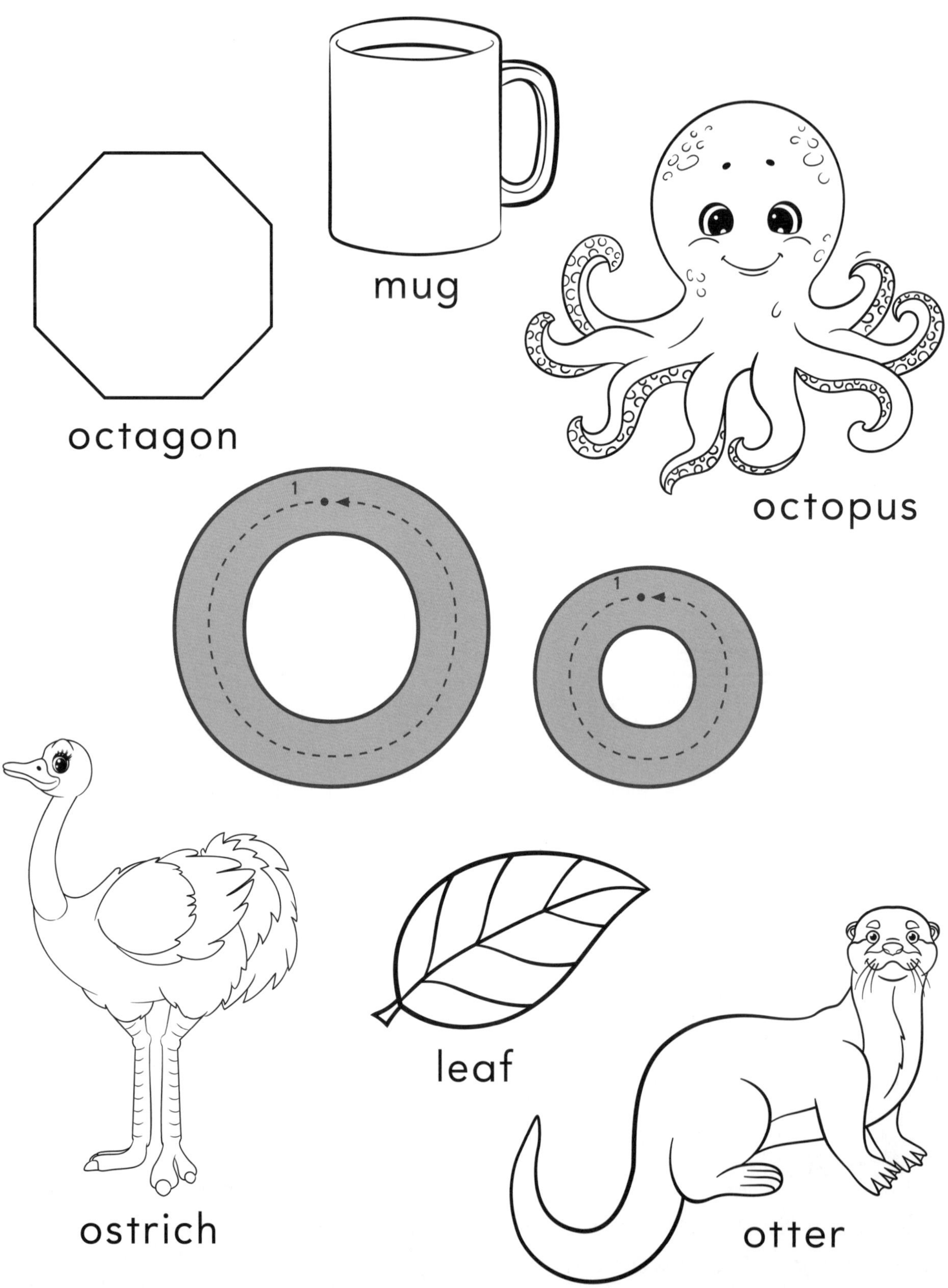

Directions: Trace the letters *O* and *o* with your finger while saying the sound /ŏ/. Name each picture. Say the first sound you hear in each word. Color the pictures that begin with the /ŏ/ sound. Write an *X* on the pictures that do not.

Name: ______________________

Directions: Trace the letters *C* and *c* with your finger while saying the sound /c/. Name each picture. Say the first sound you hear in each word. Color the pictures that begin with /c/. Draw a line connecting each picture that begins with the /c/ sound to the letters.

Name: ______________________

leaf

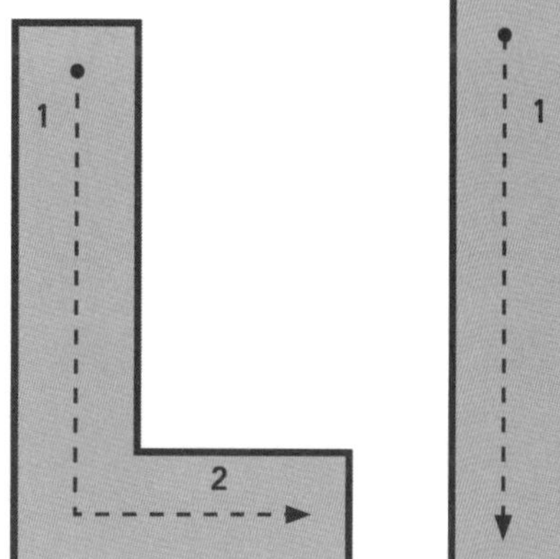

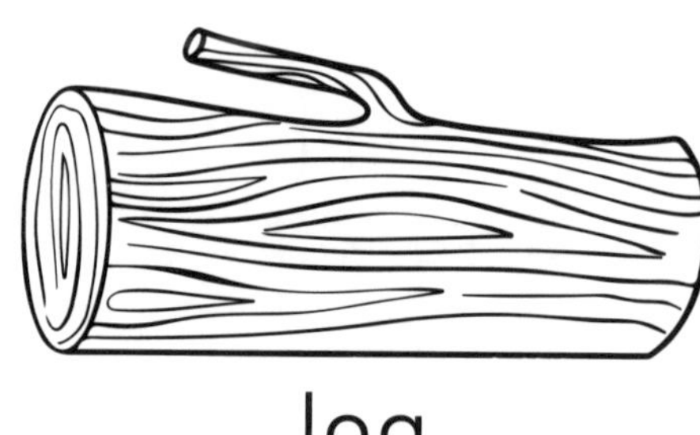

log

gift

Directions: Trace the letters *L* and *l* with your finger while saying the sound /l/. Name each picture. Say the first sound you hear in each word. Color the pictures that begin with the /l/ sound. Draw two items that begin with the /l/ sound in the box.

Name: ______________________

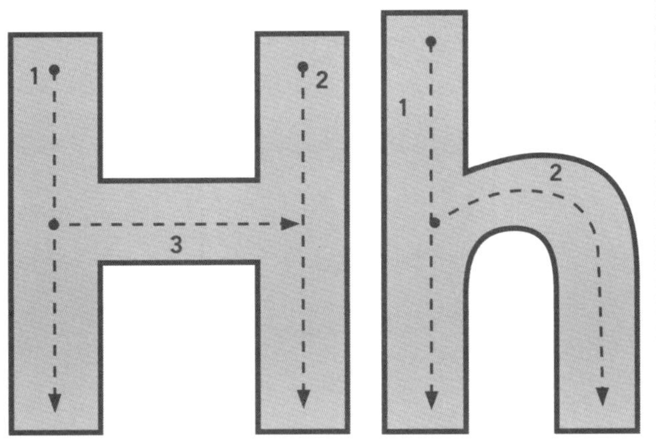

2.

1.

3.

Directions: Trace the letters *H* and *h* with your finger while saying the sound /h/. Listen as I say the sounds for the first picture. *(Say the sounds for the first picture: /h/ /ŏ/ /p/.)* Touch the dot in each box as I repeat each sound in the word. *(Repeat the sounds /h/ /ŏ/ /p/.)* Run your finger across the boxes as we say the sounds together. What word is this? *(Repeat this process for all the pictures.)* Then, color the pictures.

Name: ______________________

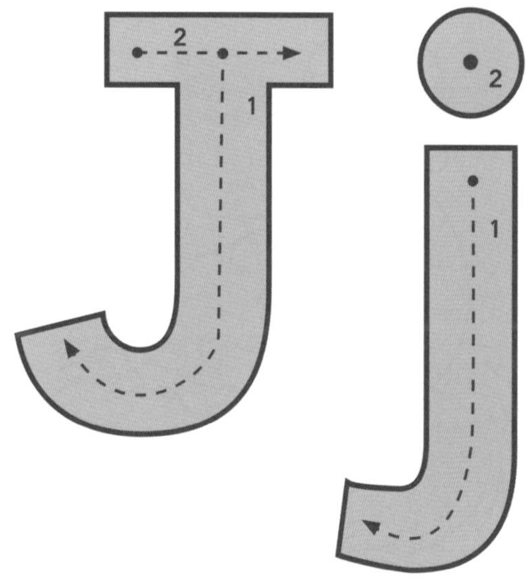

2.

1.

3.

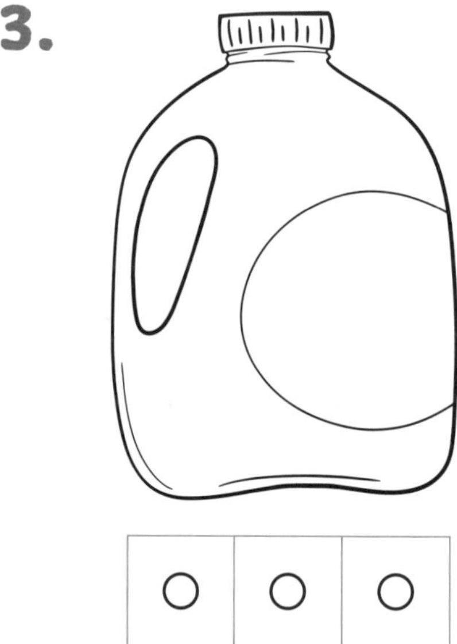

Directions: Trace the letters *J* and *j* with your finger while saying the sound /j/. Listen as I say the word and each sound in the word for the first picture. *(Say the word* jog. *Then, say it slowly, stretching out each sound: /j/ /ŏ/ /g/.)* Touch the dot in each box as you say each sound in the word. Say the word again. This time, color the dots as you repeat the sounds in each word. *(Repeat this process for all the pictures.)* Then, color the pictures.

Try This!

Draw a hopscotch grid with the letters from the unit. Take turns hopping through the grid. Say the sound for each letter as you land on it.

Overview

Short Vowel *Uu* and Consonants *Rr*, *Kk*, *Dd*, and *Yy*

Blending is the ability to combine sounds to form a word. Segmenting is the ability to break words into individual sounds. Both are prerequisite skills for learning to read. Students will practice blending and segmenting each week.

In this unit, students will learn to recognize the letters *u*, *r*, *k*, *d*, and *y* and the sounds they make. Activities for the letter *u* will focus on the short sound /ŭ/.

The letter *y* is sometimes a vowel and sometimes a consonant. When a word or syllable starts with *y*, or when there is another vowel in the word, then the *y* is usually a consonant. When *y* is a vowel, it will typically make an *e* or *i* sound, such as in *lovely* or *fry*. When it is a consonant, it makes the /y/ sound, such as in *yoyo*. In this unit, students will learn about *y* as a consonant.

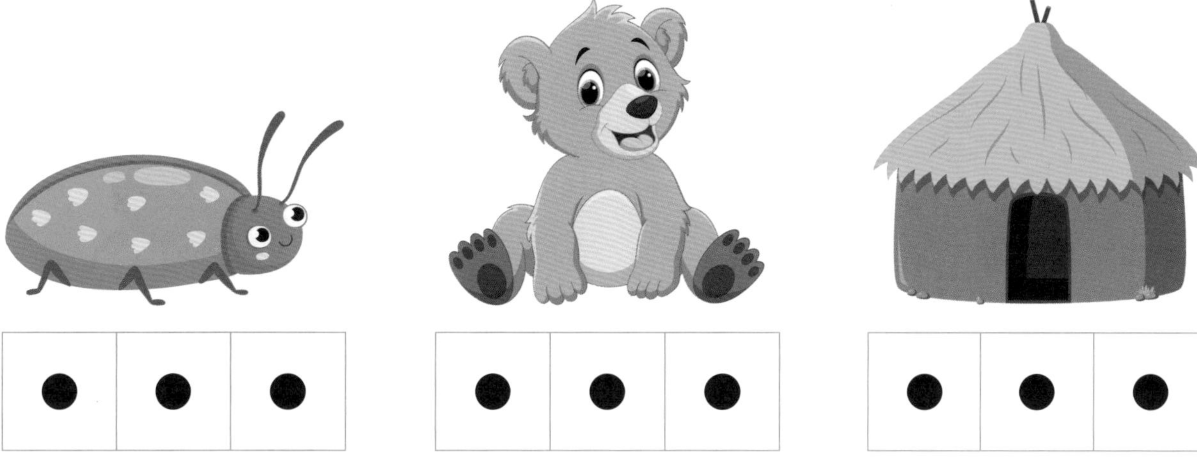

Directions: Look at the pictures. In these words, the *u* is pronounced "uh." Listen for each sound in the word. *(Slowly say the sounds for the first picture, /b/ /ŭ/ /g/, touching one dot for each sound. Then, say the word naturally.)* Touch each dot while I say the sounds again: /b/ /ŭ/ /g/. What sounds did you hear? *(Repeat this process for* cub *and* hut.*)*

Name: ______________________

umbrella

us

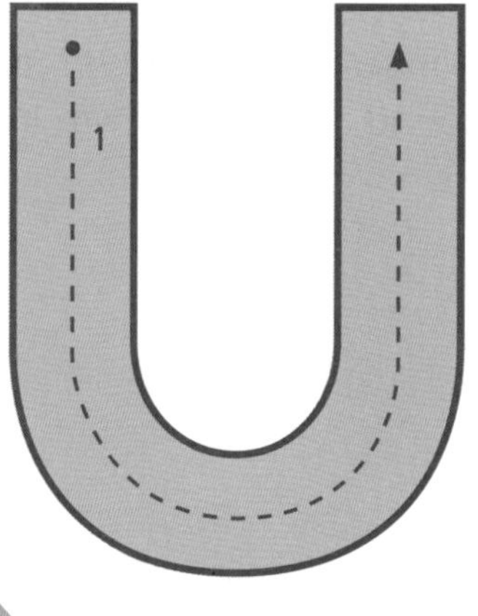

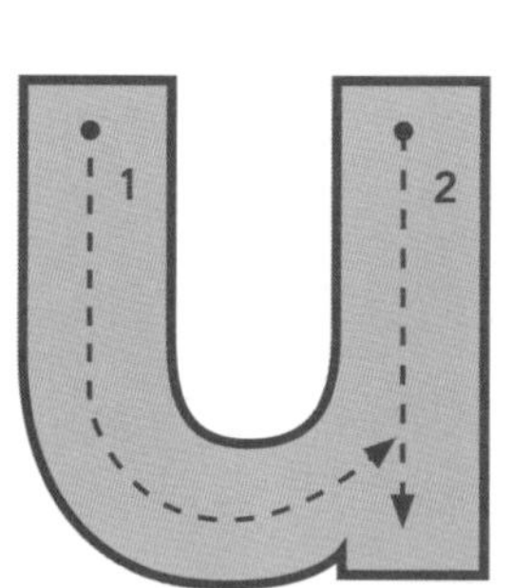

up

umpire

Directions: Trace the letters *U* and *u* with your finger while saying the sound /ŭ/. Repeat this sound while skywriting the letters. Name each picture, listening for the /ŭ/ sound. Find something around you that begins with the /ŭ/ sound. Draw it in the box.

Name: ______________________

Try This!

Fill a zip top bag halfway with hair gel or paint. Seal the bag, and tape it securely to a table. Practice writing the letters *U* and *u* on the bag. Say the /ŭ/ sound each time.

Directions: Name each picture. Say the first sound you hear in each word. Circle the picture that begins with the /ŭ/ sound. Draw an item that begins with the /ŭ/ sound in the box.

Name: ______________________

	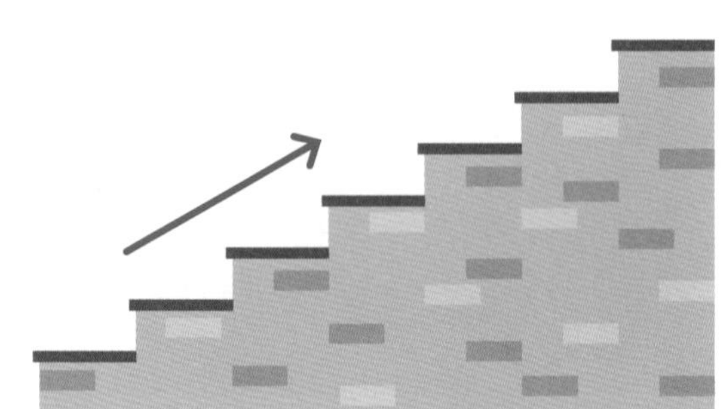

Directions: Name each picture in the table. Say the first sound you hear in each word. Circle the picture that begins with the /ŭ/ sound. Look at the pictures below. Color the image that begins with the /ŭ/ sound.

Try This!

Use a jump rope, long piece of ribbon, or bathrobe belt to make a giant letter *U*. Practice forming the letter *U* and making the /ŭ/ sound.

Name: ______________________

1.

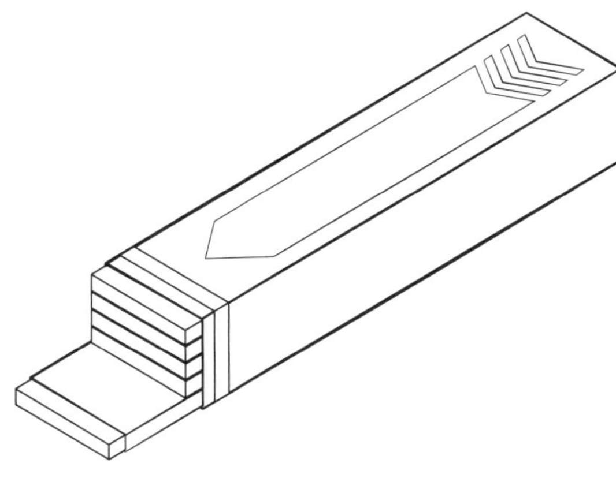

● ● ●

2.

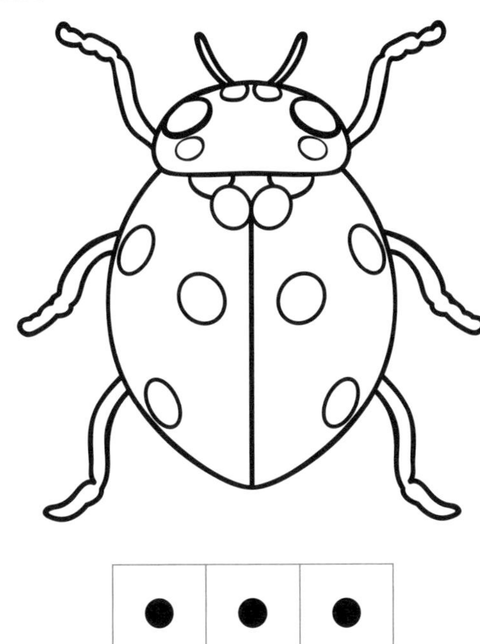

● ● ●

3.

● ● ●

4.

● ● ●

Directions: Listen as I say the sounds for the first picture. *(Say the sounds for the first picture: /g/ /ŭ/ /m/.)* Touch the dot in each box as I repeat each sound in the word. *(Repeat the sounds /g/ /ŭ/ /m/.)* Run your finger across the boxes as we say the sounds together. What word is this? *(Repeat this process for all the pictures.)* Then, color the pictures.

Name: ______________________

1.

○ ○ ○

3.

○ ○ ○

2.

○ ○ ○

4.

○ ○ ○

Directions: Listen as I say the word and each sound in the word for the first picture. *(Say the word* bun. *Then, say it slowly, stretching out each sound: /b/ /ŭ/ /n/.)* Touch the dot in each box as you say each sound in the word. Say the word again. This time, color the dots as you repeat the sounds in each word. *(Repeat this process for all the pictures.)* Then, color the pictures.

Name: ______________________

rabbit

rice

robot

rug

Directions: Trace the letters *R* and *r* with your finger while saying the sound /r/. Repeat this sound while skywriting the letters. Name each picture, listening for the /r/ sound. Find something around you that begins with the /r/ sound. Draw it in the box.

Name: ______________________

Directions: Name each picture. Say the first sound you hear in each word. Circle the picture that begins with the /r/ sound. Draw an item that begins with the /r/ sound in the box.

Try This!

Practice writing *R* and *r* using every color of the rainbow. Each time you write the letters, make the /r/ sound.

Name: ______________________________

Consonant *Rr*

Directions: Name each picture in the table. Say the first sound you hear in each word. Circle the picture that begins with the /r/ sound. Look at the pictures below. Color the images that begin with the /r/ sound.

Name: ______________________

Consonant *Rr*

1.

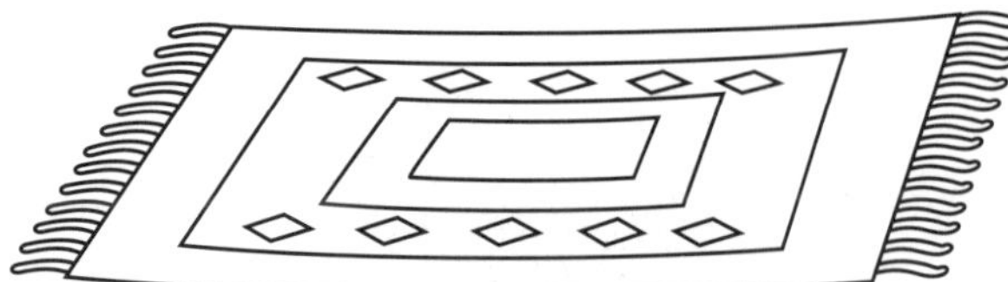

3.

2.

4.

Directions: Listen as I say the onset and rime for the first picture. *(Say the onset and rime for the first picture: /r/ /ug/.)* Touch the dot in each puzzle piece as I repeat the onset and rime in the word. *(Repeat the onset and rime /r/ /ug/.)* Run your finger across the puzzle pieces as we say the onset and rime together. What word is this? *(Repeat this process for all the pictures.)* Then, color the pictures.

Name: ____________________

1.

2.

3.

4.

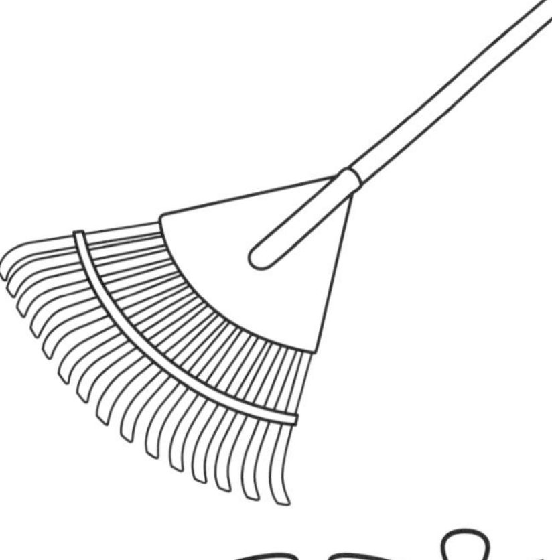

Consonant *Rr*

Directions: Listen as I say the word and the onset and rime for the first picture. *(Say the word* rice. *Then, say it slowly, stretching it out into onset and rime: /r/ /ice/.)* Touch the dot in each puzzle piece as you say the onset and rime. Say the word again. This time, color the dots as you repeat the onset and rime. *(Repeat this process for all the pictures.)* Then, color the pictures.

Name: ______________________

Directions: Trace the letters *K* and *k* with your finger while saying the sound /k/. Notice that it is the same sound that *c* makes. Repeat this sound while skywriting the letters. Name each picture, listening for the /k/ sound. Find something around you that begins with the /k/ sound. Draw it in the box.

Name: ______________________________

Try This!

Use craft sticks or cotton swabs to create four letter *K*s. Practice the /k/ sound each time you build it.

Directions: Name each picture. Say the first sound you hear in each word. Circle the picture that begins with the /k/ sound. Draw an item that begins with the /k/ sound in the box.

Name: ______________________

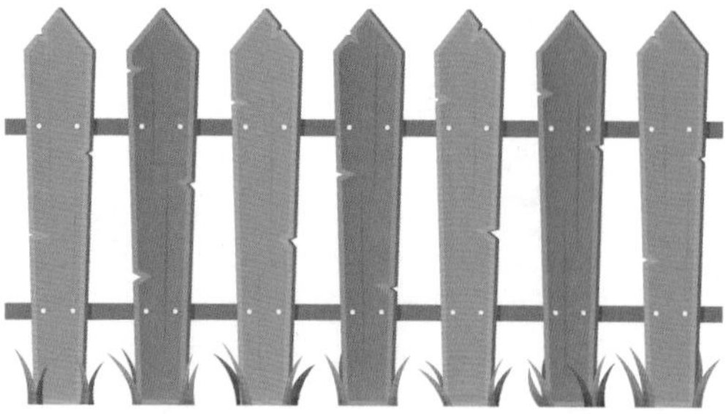

Directions: Name each picture in the table. Say the first sound you hear in each word. Circle the picture that begins with the /k/ sound. Look at the pictures below. Color the image that begins with the /k/ sound.

Name: ____________________

1.

2.

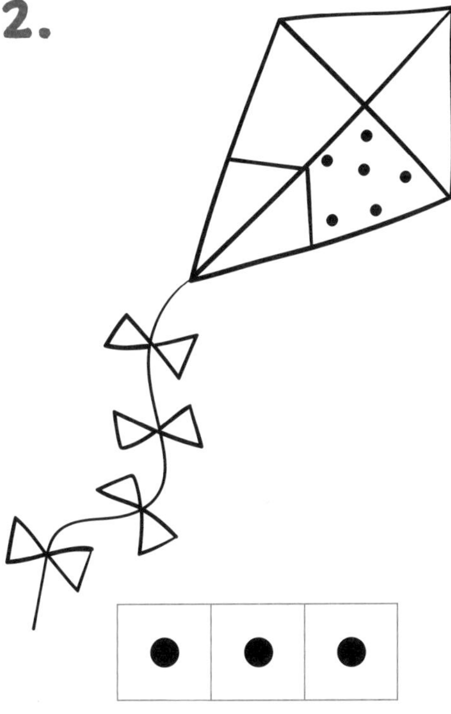

3.

4.

Directions: Listen as I say the sounds for the first picture. *(Say the sounds for the first picture: /k/ /ĭ/ /d/.)* Touch the dot in each box as I repeat each sound in the word. *(Repeat the sounds /k/ /ĭ/ /d/.)* Run your finger across the boxes as we say the sounds together. What word is this? *(Repeat this process for all the pictures.)* Then, color the pictures.

Name: ____________________

1.

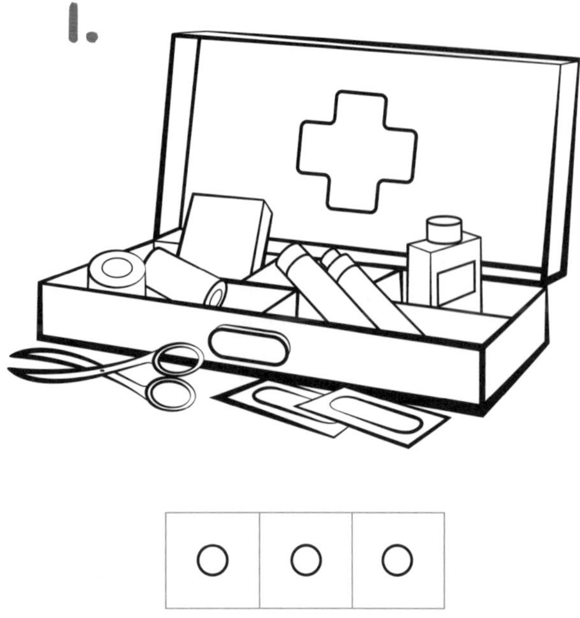

○ ○ ○

2.

○ ○ ○

3.

○ ○ ○

4.

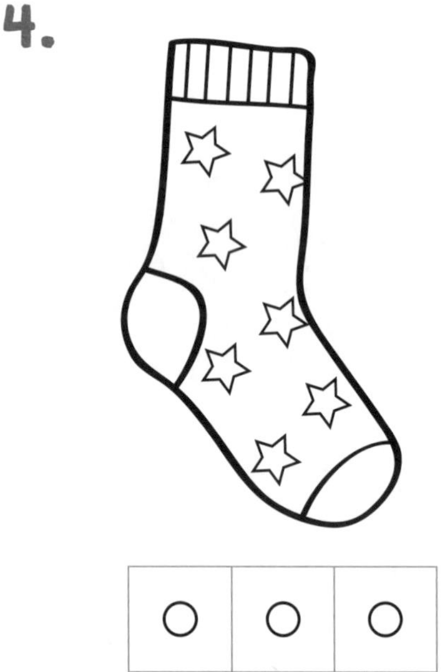

○ ○ ○

Directions: Listen as I say the word and each sound in the word for the first picture. *(Say the word* kit. *Then, say it slowly, stretching out each sound: /k/ /ĭ/ /t/.)* Touch the dot in each box as you say each sound in the word. Say the word again. This time, color the dots as you repeat the sounds in each word. *(Repeat this process for all the pictures.)* Then, color the pictures.

Try This!

Play Head, Shoulders, Knees, and Toes as you segment the words. As you say the sounds in each word, touch your head, shoulders, and knees.

Name: ____________________

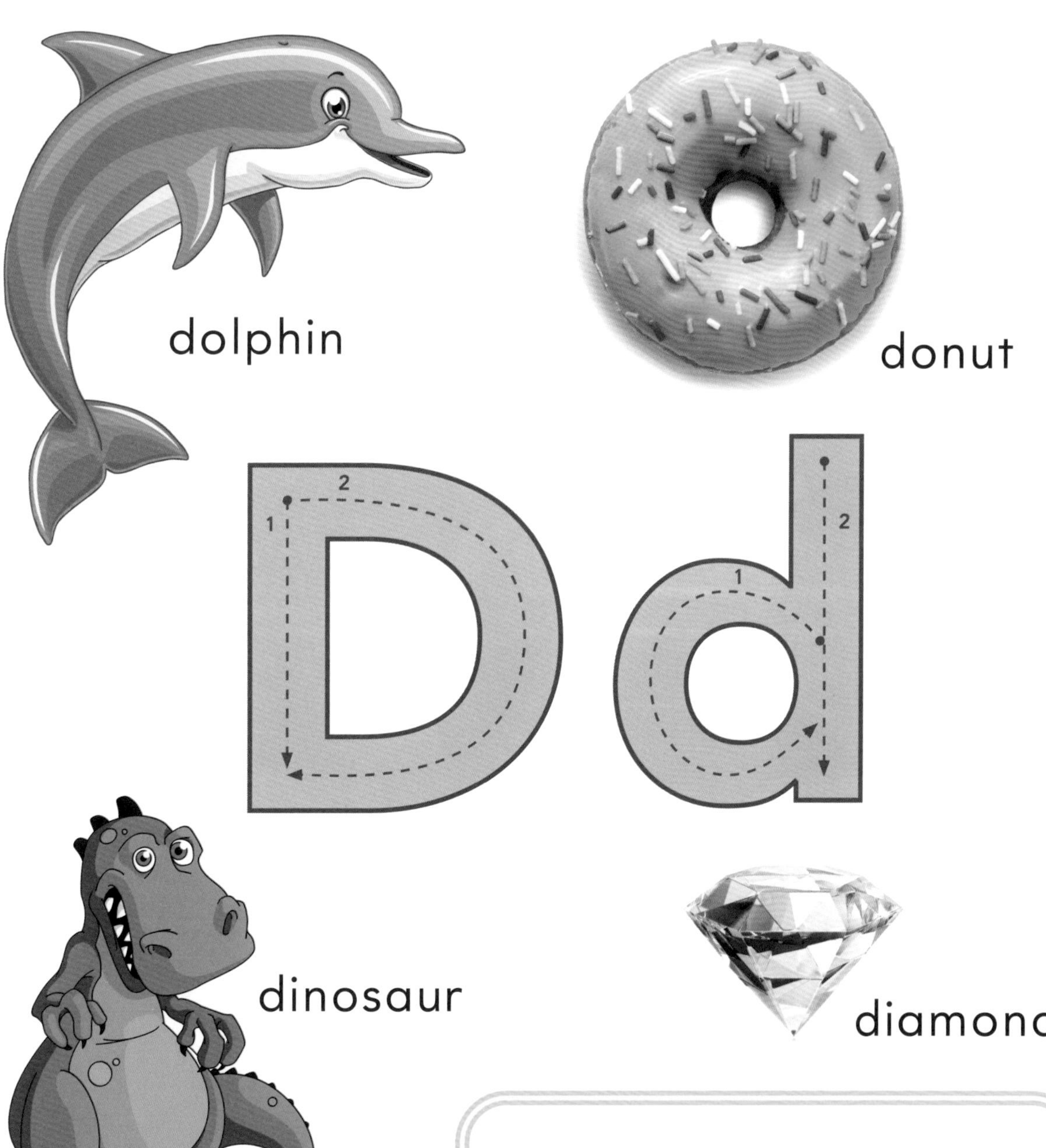

Directions: Trace the letters *D* and *d* with your finger while saying the sound /d/. Repeat this sound while skywriting the letters. Name each picture, listening for the /d/ sound. Find something around you that begins with the /d/ sound. Draw it in the box.

Name: ____________________

Directions: Name each picture. Say the first sound you hear in each word. Circle the picture that begins with the /d/ sound. Draw an item that begins with the /d/ sound in the box.

Name: ______________________

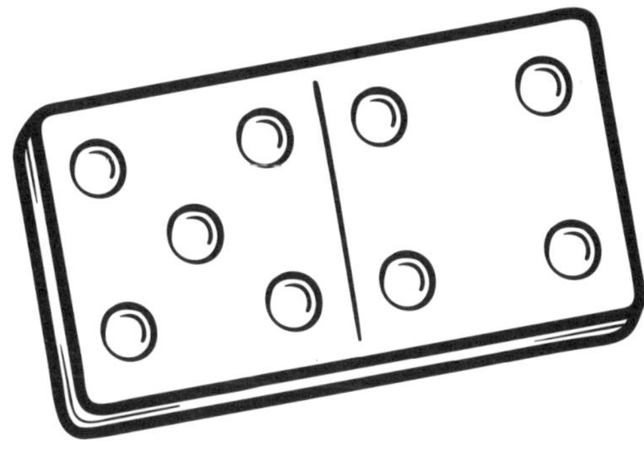

Directions: Name each picture in the table. Say the first sound you hear in each word. Circle the picture that begins with the /d/ sound. Look at the pictures below. Color the images that begin with the /d/ sound.

Name: ______________________

1.

3.

2.

4.

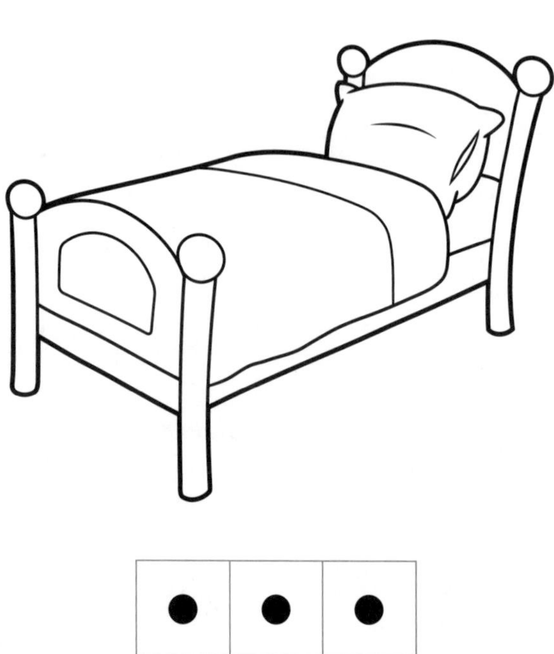

Directions: Listen as I say the sounds for the first picture. *(Say the sounds for the first picture: /d/ /ŏ/ /g/.)* Touch the dot in each box as I repeat each sound in the word. *(Repeat the sounds /d/ /ŏ/ /g/.)* Run your finger across the boxes as we say the sounds together. What word is this? *(Repeat this process for all the pictures:* den, duck, *and* bed.*)* Then, color the pictures.

Name: ______________________

1.

○ ○ ○

2.

○ ○ ○

3.

○ ○ ○

4.

○ ○ ○

Try This!

Move your body to segment the words. Stomp your foot, jump, or hop for each sound you hear.

Directions: Listen as I say the word and each sound in the word for the first picture. *(Say the word* dig. *Then, say it slowly, stretching out each sound: /d/ /ĭ/ /g/.)* Touch the dot in each box as you say each sound in the word. Say the word again. This time, color the dots as you repeat the sounds in each word. *(Repeat this process for all the pictures.)* Then, color the pictures.

Name: ____________________

Consonant *Yy*

yogurt

yoyo

yarn

yoga

Directions: Trace the letters *Y* and *y* with your finger while saying the sound /y/. Repeat this sound while skywriting the letters. Name each picture, listening for the /y/ sound. Find something around you that begins with the /y/ sound. Draw it in the box.

Name: ______________________

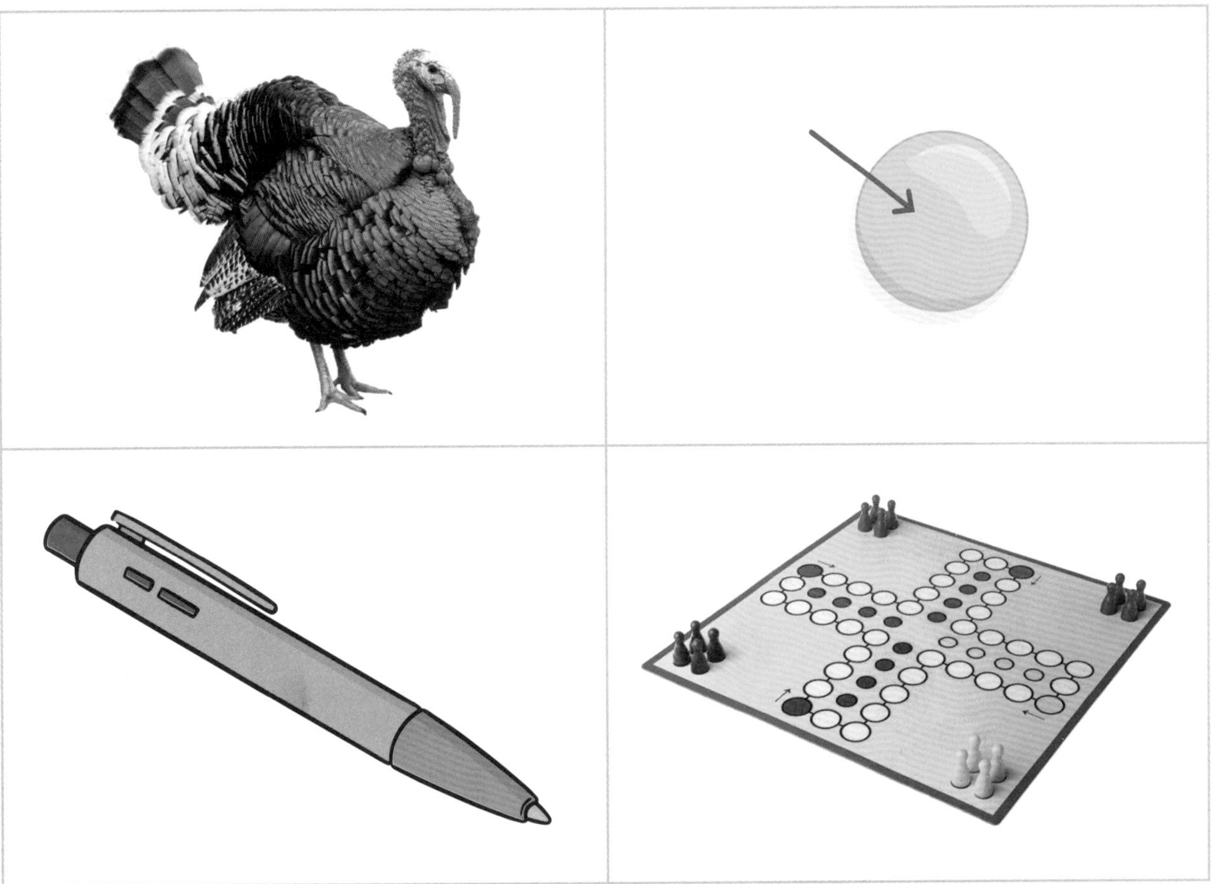

Consonant Yy

Try This!

Use masking tape to create a letter *Y* on the floor. Place small blocks or toys and build on top of the letter. Practice making the /y/ sound.

Directions: Name each picture. Say the first sound you hear in each word. Circle the picture that begins with the /y/ sound. Draw an item that begins with the /y/ sound in the box.

Name: ______________________

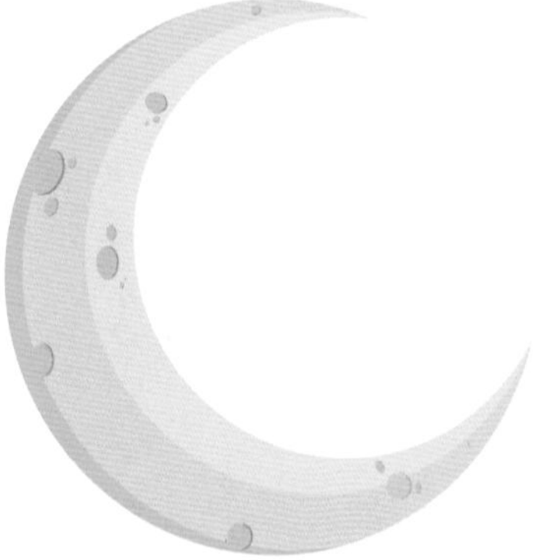

Try This!

Set up a sensory bin with rice, beans, or sand. Within the bin, hide letter *Y* beads or tiles along with objects or pictures that start with *Y*. Pull items out of the bin, and say the /y/ sound.

Directions: Name each picture in the table. Say the first sound you hear in each word. Circle the picture that begins with the /y/ sound. Look at the pictures below. Color the image that begins with the /y/ sound.

Name: ______________________

1.

3.

2.

4.

Directions: Listen as I say the sounds for the first picture. *(Say the sounds for the first picture: /y/ /ĕ/ /s/.)* Touch the dot in each box as I repeat each sound in the word. *(Repeat the sounds /y/ /ĕ/ /s/.)* Run your finger across the boxes as we say the sounds together. What word is this? *(Repeat this process for all the pictures:* yum, yak, *and* yell.*)* Then, color the pictures.

Name: ____________________

1.

○	○	○

2.

○	○	○

3.

○	○	○	○

4.

○	○	○	○

Directions: Listen as I say the word and each sound in the word for the first picture. *(Say the word* yam. *Then, say it slowly, stretching out each sound: /y/ /ă/ /m/.)* Touch the dot in each box as you say each sound in the word. Say the word again. This time, color the dots as you repeat the sounds in each word. *(Repeat this process for all the pictures.)* Then, color the pictures.

Name: ______________________

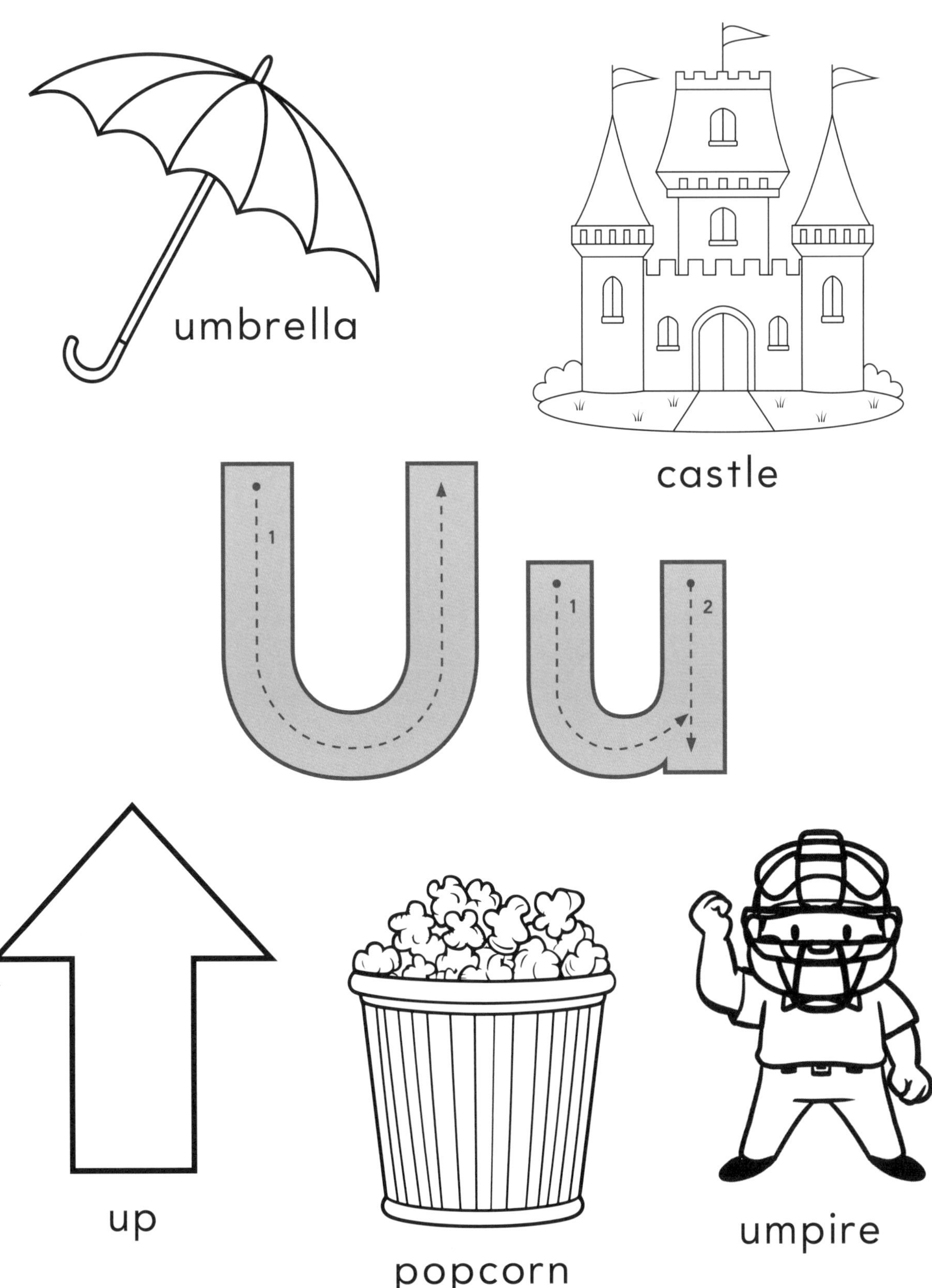

Directions: Trace the letters *U* and *u* with your finger while saying the sound /ŭ/. Name each picture. Say the first sound you hear in each word. Color the pictures that begin with the /ŭ/ sound. Write an *X* on the pictures that do not.

Name: ____________________

Review: *Uu, Rr, Kk, Dd, Yy*

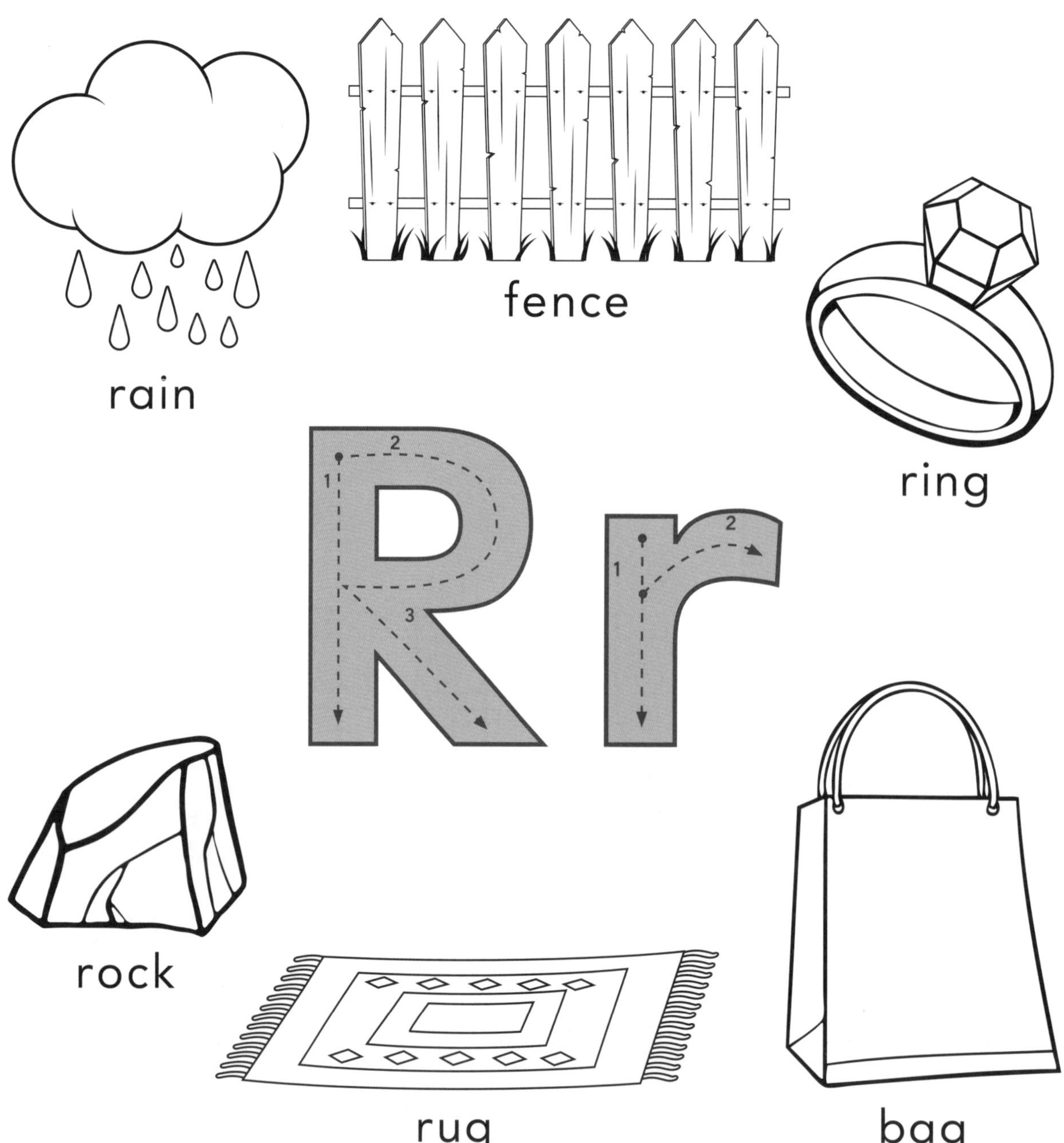

Directions: Trace the letters *R* and *r* with your finger while saying the sound /r/. Name each picture. Say the first sound you hear in each word. Color the pictures that begin with /r/. Draw a line connecting each picture that begins with the /r/ sound to the letters *R* and *r*.

Try This!

Fill a zip top bag halfway with hair gel or paint. Seal the bag, and tape it securely to a table. Practice writing the letters from this unit on the bag. Make the letter sound each time you write one.

Name: ____________________

Directions: Trace the letters *K* and *k* with your finger while saying the sound /k/. Name each picture. Say the first sound you hear in each word. Color the pictures that begin with the /k/ sound. Draw two items that begin with the /k/ sound in the box.

Name: ____________________

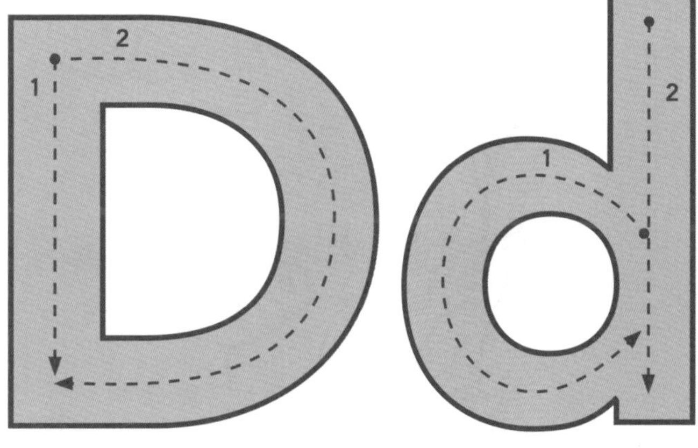

2.

1.

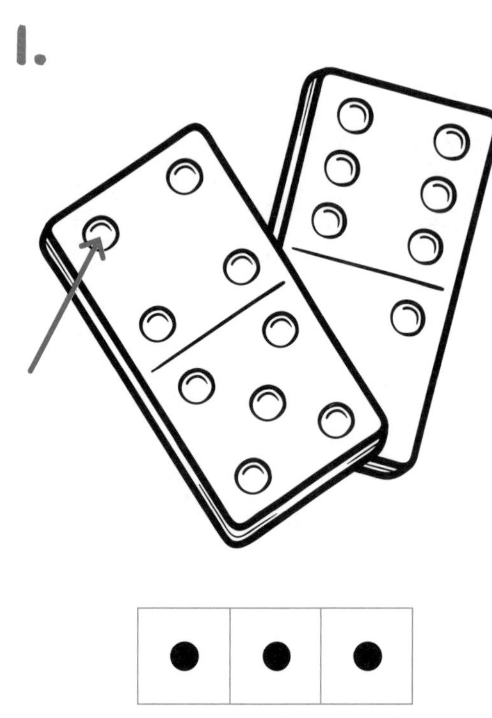

3.

Directions: Trace the letters *D* and *d* with your finger while saying the sound /d/. Listen as I say the sounds for the first picture. *(Say the sounds for the first picture: /d/ /ŏ/ /t/.)* Touch the dot in each box as I repeat each sound in the word. *(Repeat the sounds /d/ /ŏ/ /t/.)* Run your finger across the boxes as we say the sounds together. What word is this? *(Repeat this process for all the pictures.)* Then, color the pictures.

Name: ________________________

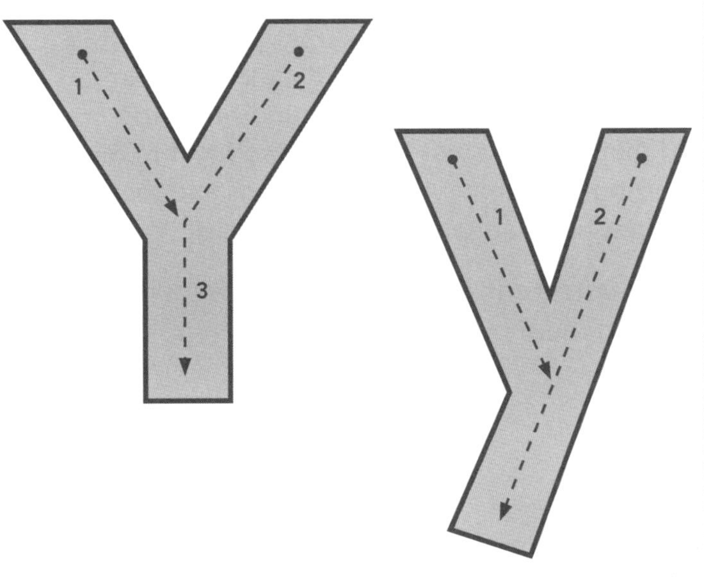

2.

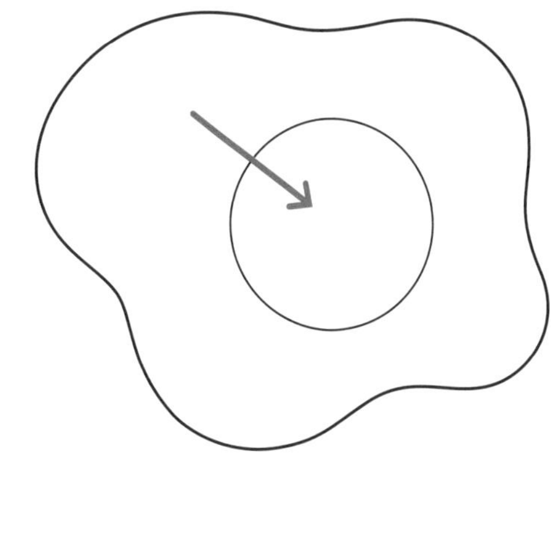

1.

3.

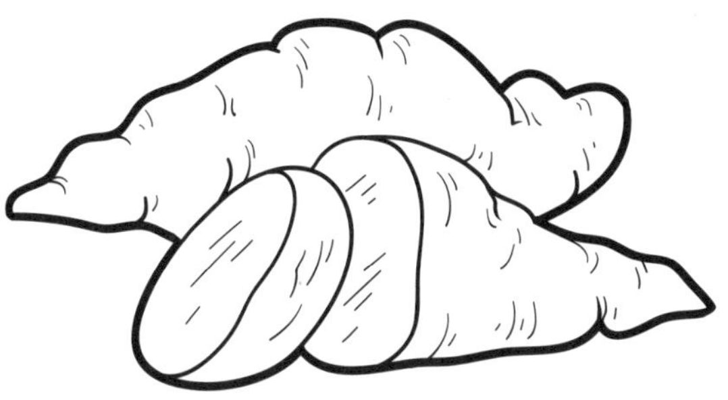

Directions: Trace the letters *Y* and *y* with your finger while saying the sound /y/. Listen as I say the word and each sound in the word for the first picture. *(Say the word* yes. *Then, say it slowly, stretching out each sound: /y/ /ĕ/ /s/.)* Touch the dot in each box as you say each sound in the word. Say the word again. This time, color the dots as you repeat the sounds in each word. *(Repeat this process for all the pictures.)* Then, color the pictures.

Overview

Short Vowel *Ee* and Consonants *Qq*, *Ww*, *Vv*, *Xx*, and *Zz*

Phoneme isolation is the ability to identify phonemes (or sounds) and their locations in words. It requires listening to, recognizing, and identifying individual sounds in words. Learners begin with isolating the first sound they hear in a word and connecting it to the printed letter. They then move on to recognizing and identifying final sounds and then medial sounds. Students will have opportunities to isolate phonemes each week.

In this unit, students will learn to recognize the letters *e*, *q*, *w*, *v*, *x*, and *z* and the sounds they make. Activities for the letter *e* will focus on the short sound /ĕ/.

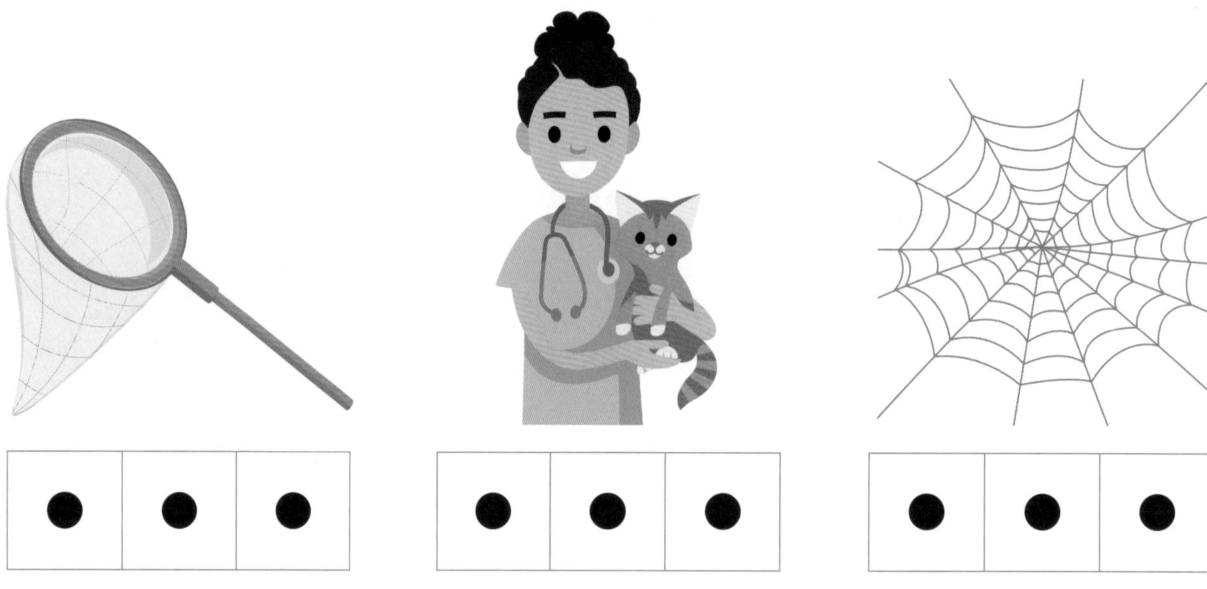

Directions: Look at the pictures. In these words, the *e* is pronounced "eh." Listen for each sound in the word. *(Slowly say the sounds for the first picture, /n/ /ĕ/ /t/, touching one dot for each sound. Then, say the word naturally.)* Touch each dot while I say the sounds again: /n/ /ĕ/ /t/. What was the first sound you heard? What was the last sound you heard? *(Repeat this process for* vet *and* web.*)*

Name: ______________________________

egg

Directions: Trace the letters *E* and *e* with your finger while saying the sound /ĕ/. Repeat this sound while skywriting the letters. Name each picture, listening for the /ĕ/ sound. Find something around you that begins with the /ĕ/ sound. Draw it in the box.

Name: ____________________

Directions: Name each picture. Say the first sound you hear in each word. Circle the picture that begins with the /ĕ/ sound. Draw an item that begins with the /ĕ/ sound in the box.

Try This!

Spread a thin layer of shaving foam on a cookie sheet. Practice writing the letters *E* and *e* with your finger or a craft stick. Practice the /ĕ/ sound each time you write it.

Name: ____________________

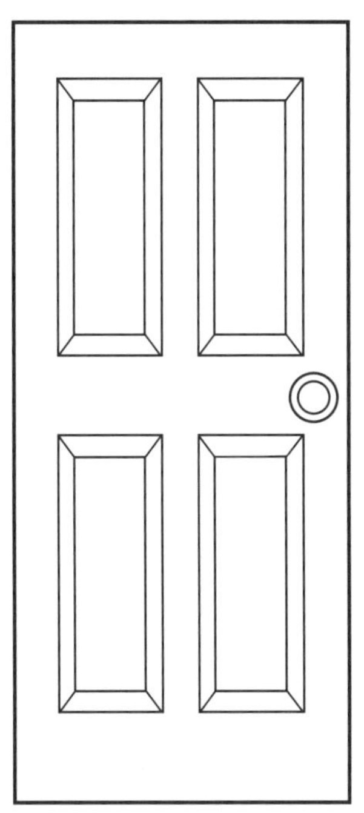

Directions: Name each picture in the table. Say the first sound you hear in each word. Circle the picture that begins with the /ĕ/ sound. Look at the pictures below. Color the image that begins with the /ĕ/ sound.

Name: ______________________

1.

3.

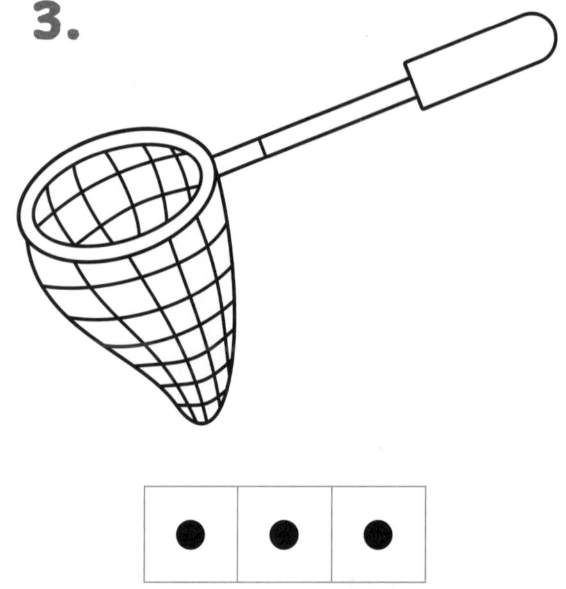

2.

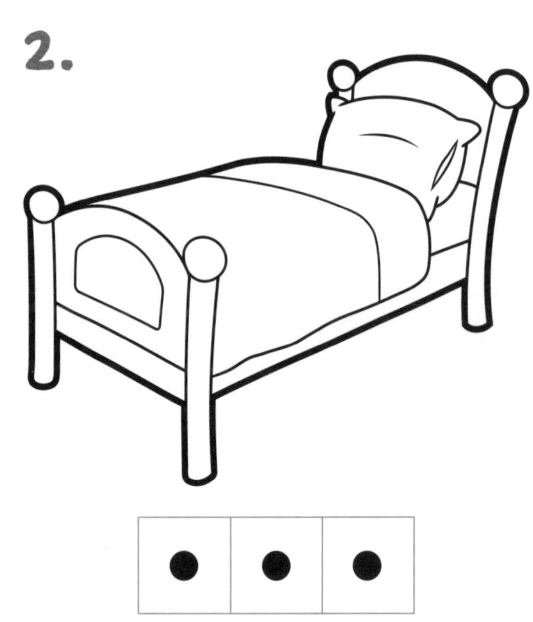

4.

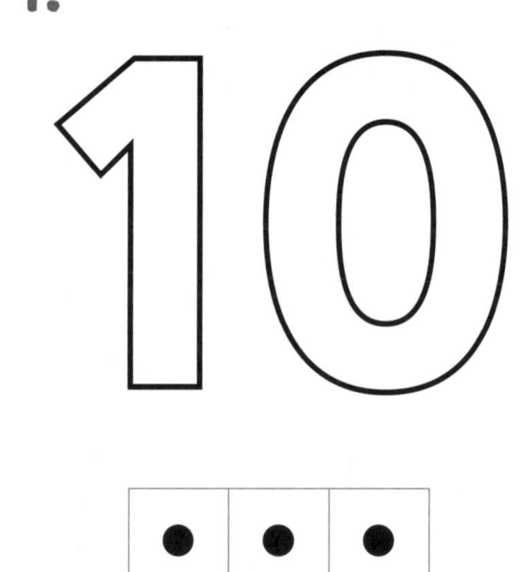

Directions: Listen as I say the sounds for the first picture. *(Say the sounds for the first picture: /h/ /ĕ/ /n/.)* Touch the dot in each box as I repeat each sound in the word. *(Repeat the sounds /h/ /ĕ/ /n/.)* Run your finger across the boxes as we say the sounds together. What word is this? *(Repeat this process for all the pictures.)* Then, color the pictures.

Try This!

Use your arm to tap out the sounds you hear in the word. Tap your shoulder for the first sound, elbow for the second sound, and hand for the third sound.

Name: ______________________________

1.

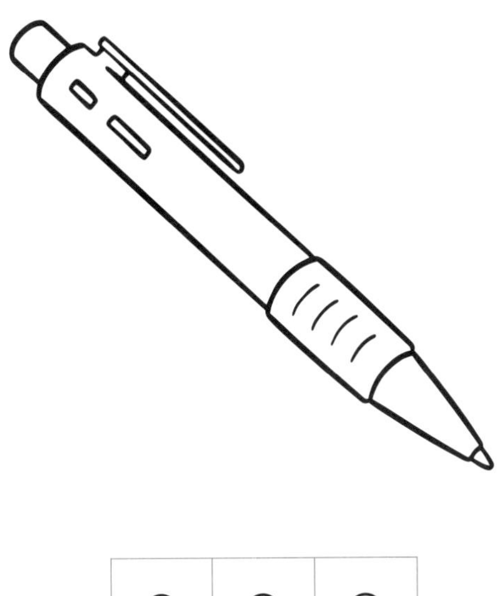

3.

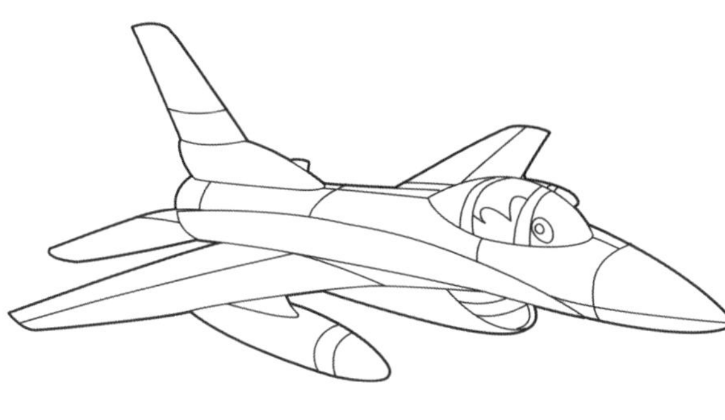

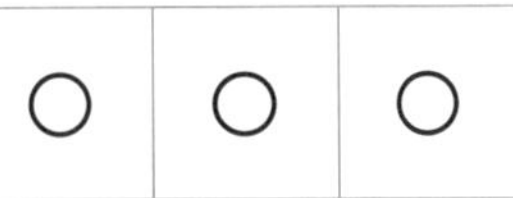

2.

4.

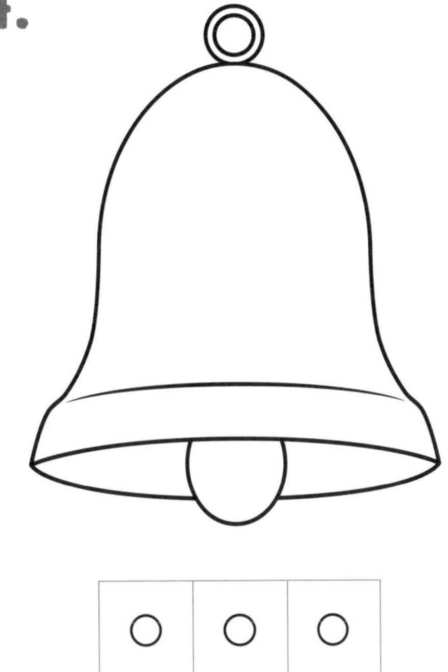

Directions: Listen as I say the word and each sound in the word for the first picture. *(Say the word* pen. *Then, say it slowly, stretching out each sound: /p/ /ĕ/ /n/.)* Touch the dot in each box as you say each sound in the word. Say the word again. This time, color the dots as you repeat the sounds in each word. *(Repeat this process for all the pictures.)* Then, color the pictures.

Name: ______________________

Consonant *Qq*

quail

quilt

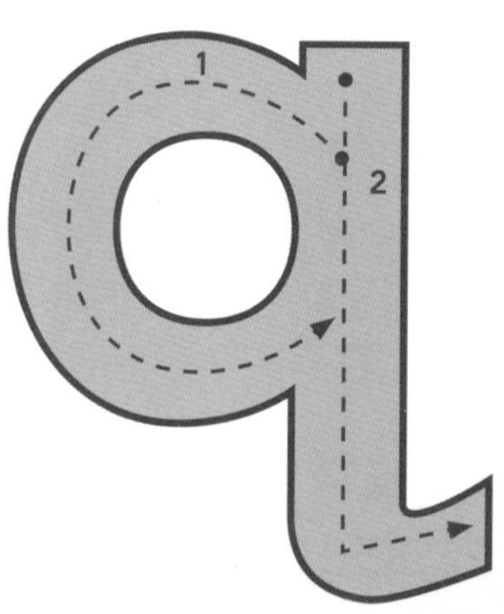

quarter

queen

Directions: Trace the letters *Q* and *q* with your finger while saying the sound /qu/. Repeat this sound while skywriting the letters. Name each picture, listening for the /qu/ sound. Find something around you that begins with the /qu/ sound. Draw it in the box.

Name: ______________________________

Directions: Name each picture. Say the first sound you hear in each word. Circle the picture that begins with the /qu/ sound. Draw an item that begins with the /qu/ sound in the box.

Name: ____________________

Directions: Name each picture in the table. Say the first sound you hear in each word. Circle the picture that begins with the /qu/ sound. Look at the pictures below. Color the image that begins with the /qu/ sound.

Name: ____________________

1.

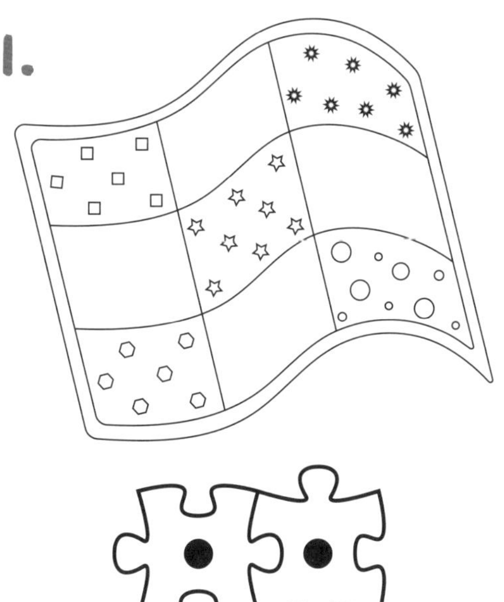

3.

2.

4.

Try This!

Stomp your left foot for the onset of each word and your right foot for the rime. Jump with your feet together when you blend to make the whole word.

Directions: Listen as I say the onset and rime for the first picture. *(Say the onset and rime for the first picture: /qu/ /ilt/.)* Touch the dot in each puzzle piece as I repeat the onset and rime in the word. *(Repeat the onset and rime /qu/ /ilt/.)* Run your finger across the puzzle pieces as we say the onset and rime together. What word is this? *(Repeat this process for all the pictures.)* Then, color the pictures.

Name: ______________________

1.

3.

2.

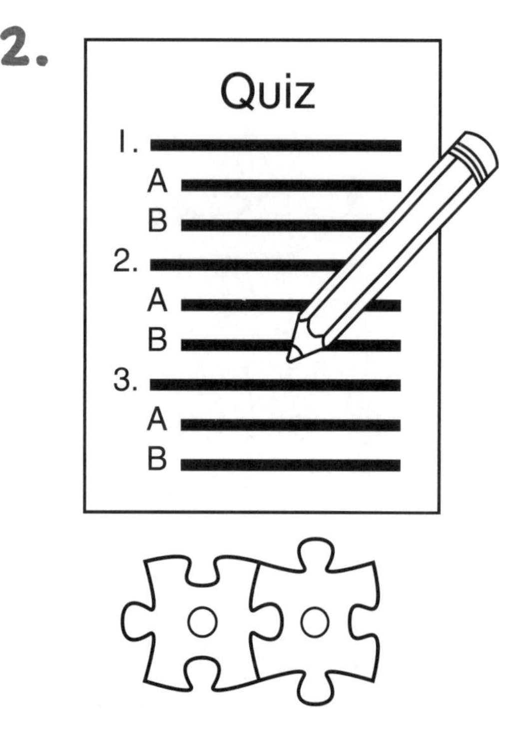

4.

Directions: Listen as I say the word and the onset and rime for the first picture. *(Say the word* quill. *Then, say it slowly, stretching it out into onset and rime: /qu/ /ill/.)* Touch the dot in each puzzle piece as you say the onset and rime. Say the word again. This time, color the dots as you repeat the onset and rime. *(Repeat this process for all the pictures:* quiz, quarter, *and* question.*)* Then, color the pictures.

Name: ____________________

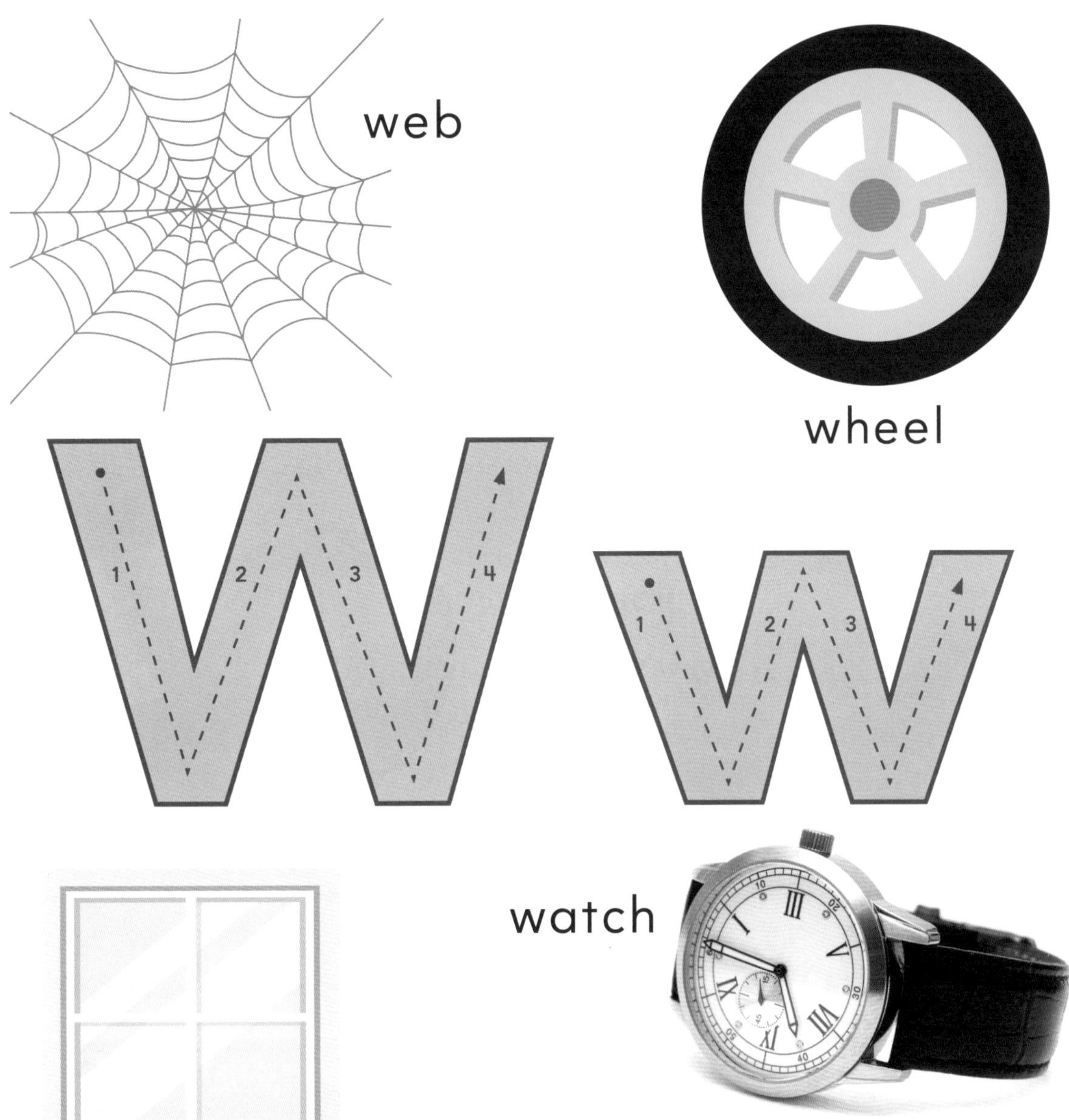

watch

window

Consonant Ww

Directions: Trace the letters *W* and *w* with your finger while saying the sound /w/. Repeat this sound while skywriting the letters. Name each picture, listening for the /w/ sound. Find something around you that begins with the /w/ sound. Draw it in the box.

Name: ________________________

Directions: Name each picture. Say the first sound you hear in each word. Circle the picture that begins with the /w/ sound. Draw an item that begins with the /w/ sound in the box.

Name: ______________________

Directions: Name each picture in the table. Say the first sound you hear in each word. Circle the picture that begins with the /w/ sound. Look at the pictures below. Color the image that begins with the /w/ sound.

Name: ______________________

1.

3.

2.

4.

Directions: Listen as I say the sounds for the first picture. *(Say the sounds for the first picture: /w/ /ĕ/ /b/.)* Touch the dot in each box as I repeat each sound in the word. *(Repeat the sounds /w/ /ĕ/ /b/.)* Run your finger across the boxes as we say the sounds together. What word is this? *(Repeat this process for all the pictures:* wag, wake, *and* win.*)* Then, color the pictures.

Name: ______________________________

1.

○ ○ ○

3.

○ ○ ○

2.

○ ○ ○

4.

SUN	MON	TUE	WED	THU	FRI	SAT
		1	2	3	4	5
6	7	8	9	10	11	12
13	14	15	16	17	18	19
20	21	22	23	24	25	26
27	28	29	30	31		

○ ○ ○

Directions: Listen as I say the word and each sound in the word for the first picture. *(Say the word* wig. *Then, say it slowly, stretching out each sound: /w/ /ĭ/ /g/.)* Touch the dot in each box as you say each sound in the word. Say the word again. This time, color the dots as you repeat the sounds in each word. *(Repeat this process for all the pictures.)* Then, color the pictures.

Name: ______________________________

Consonant *Vv*

vegetables

vest

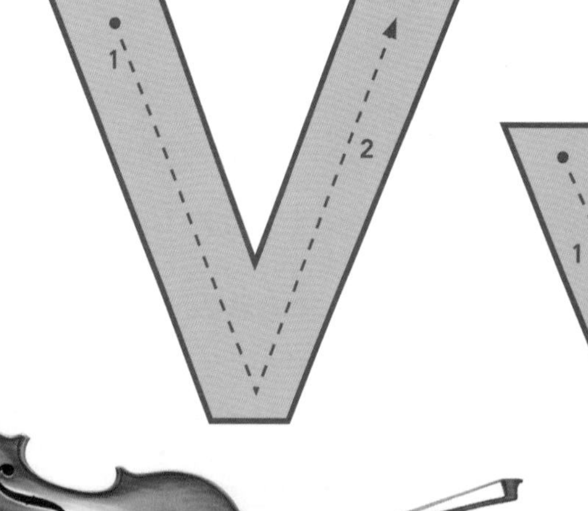

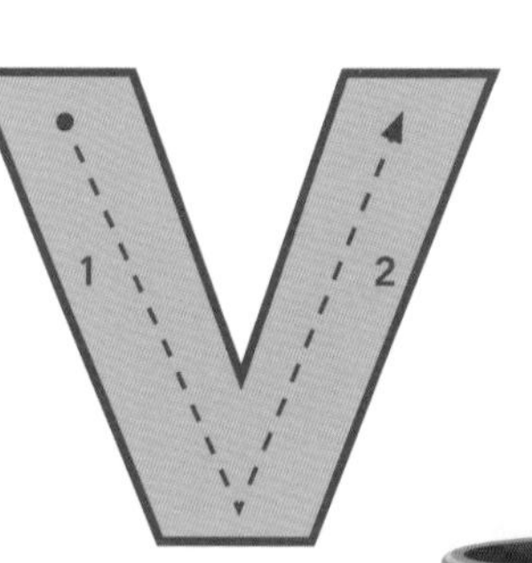

violin

vase

Directions: Trace the letters *V* and *v* with your finger while saying the sound /v/. Repeat this sound while skywriting the letters. Name each picture, listening for the /v/ sound. Find something around you that begins with the /v/ sound. Draw it in the box.

Name: ______________________

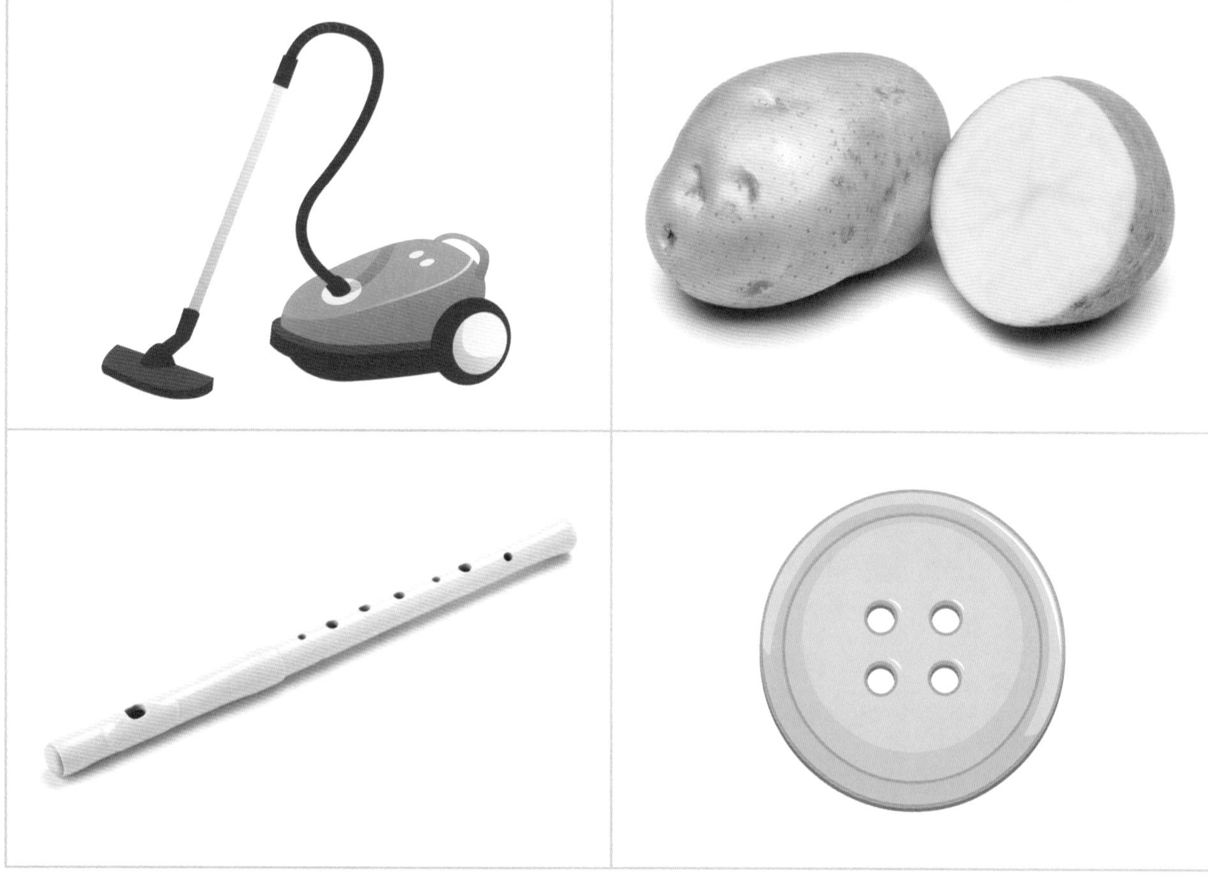

Try This!

Write *Vv* in the middle of a sheet of paper. Draw pictures of items that start with *V*. Draw lines connecting each item to the letters. As you draw, practice saying the /v/ sound.

Directions: Name each picture. Say the first sound you hear in each word. Circle the picture that begins with the /v/ sound. Draw an item that begins with the /v/ sound in the box.

Name: ____________________

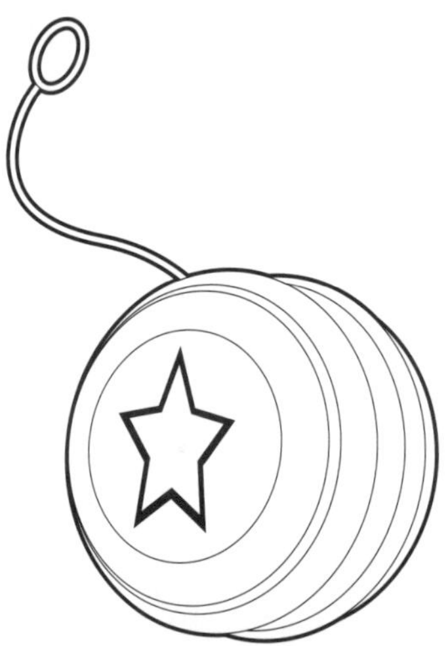

Directions: Name each picture in the table. Say the first sound you hear in each word. Circle the picture that begins with the /v/ sound. Look at the pictures below. Color the image that begins with the /v/ sound.

Try This!

Draw or write a list of your favorite vegetables. Say the initial sound of each vegetable on your list.

Name: ______________________

1.

● ● ●

3.

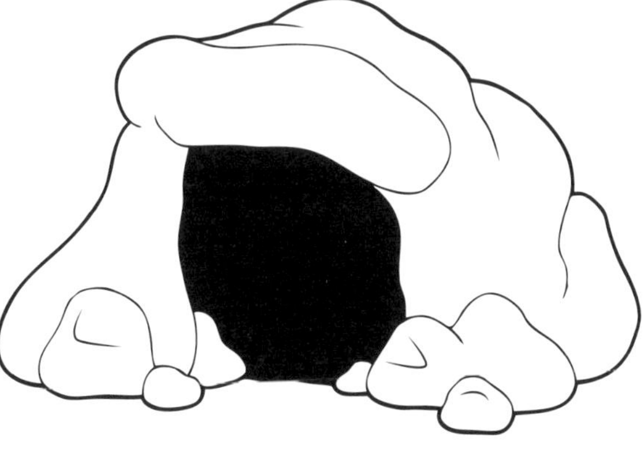

2.

● ● ●

4.

● ● ●

Directions: Listen as I say the sounds for the first picture. *(Say the sounds for the first picture: /v/ /ă/ /n/.)* Touch the dot in each box as I repeat each sound in the word. *(Repeat the sounds /v/ /ă/ /n/.)* Run your finger across the boxes as we say the sounds together. What word is this? *(Repeat this process for all the pictures.)* Then, color the pictures.

Name: ______________________

1.

○	○	○

2.

○	○	○

3.

○	○	○

4.

○	○	○

Directions: Listen as I say the word and each sound in the word for the first picture. *(Say the word* vase. *Then, say it slowly, stretching out each sound: /v/ /ā/ /s/.)* Touch the dot in each box as you say each sound in the word. Say the word again. This time, color the dots as you repeat the sounds in each word. *(Repeat this process for all the pictures:* vine, wave, *and* dove.*)* Then, color the pictures.

Name: ______________________

box

fox

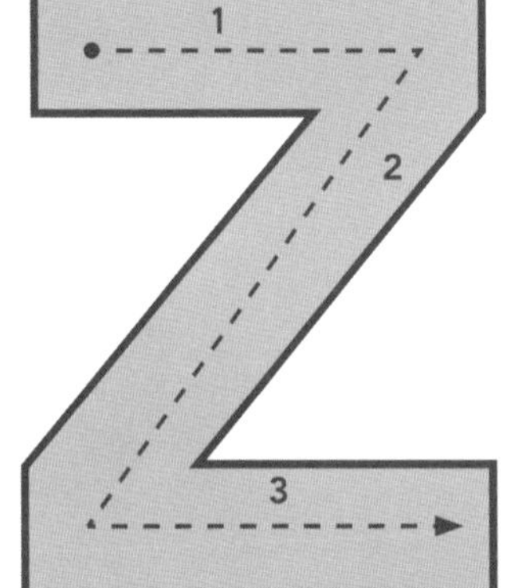

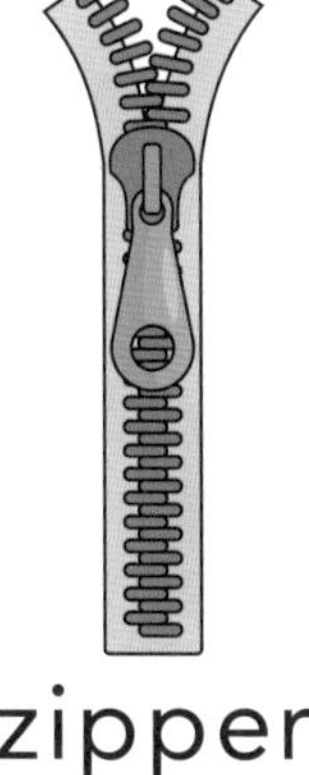

zebra

zipper

Directions: Trace the letters *X* and *x* with your finger while saying the sound /x/. Repeat this sound while skywriting the letters. Name each picture, listening for the /x/ sound. Find something around you that has the /x/ sound. Draw it in the first box. *(Repeat the activities with the letters* Z *and* z.*)*

Name: ____________________

Directions: Name each picture. Say the final sound you hear in each word. Circle the picture that ends with the /x/ sound. Draw one item that ends with the /x/ sound in the box.

Try This!

Use masking tape to create large letter Xs and letter Zs on the floor. Drive a toy car on the letters while you practice saying the sounds.

Name: ______________________

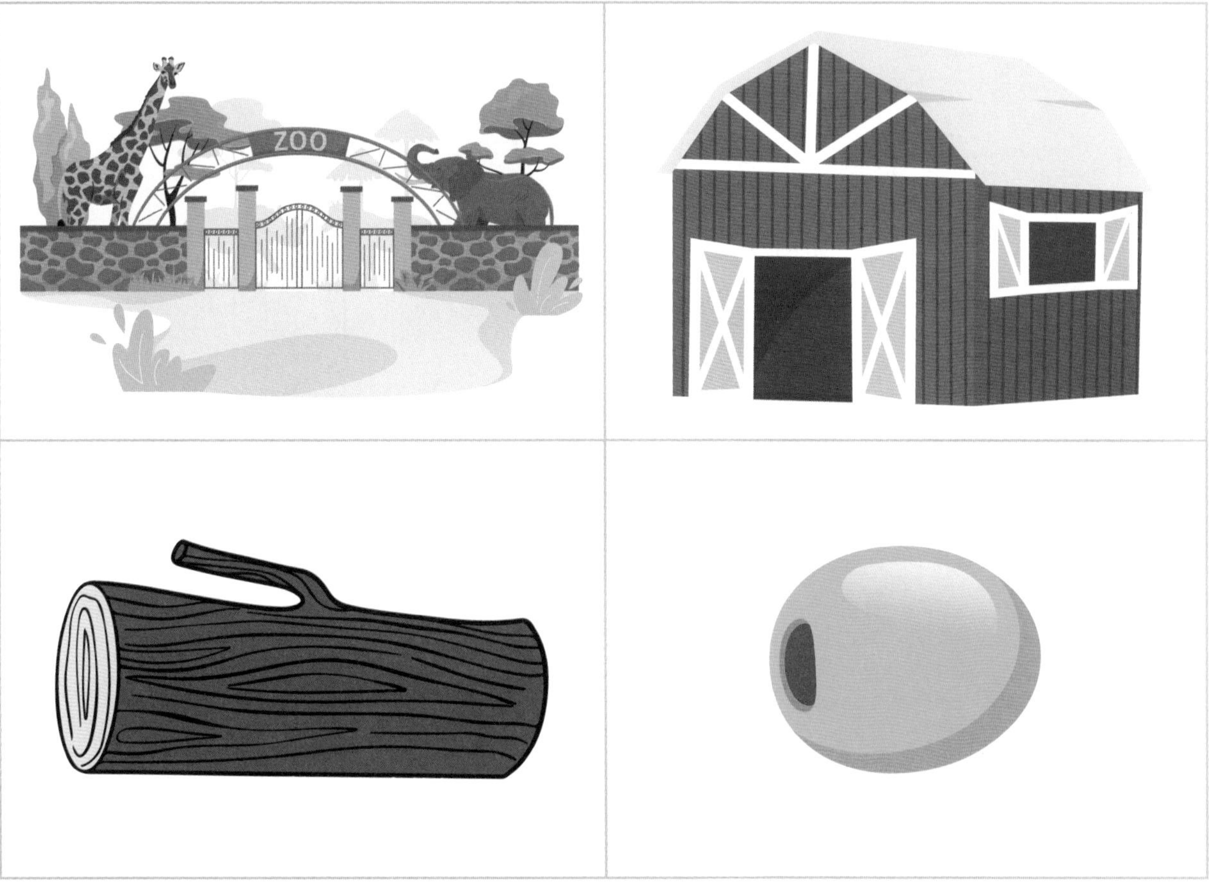

Consonants Xx and Zz

Directions: Name each picture. Say the first sound you hear in each word. Circle the picture that begins with the /z/ sound. Draw an item that begins with the /z/ sound in the box.

Name: ______________________

1.

3.

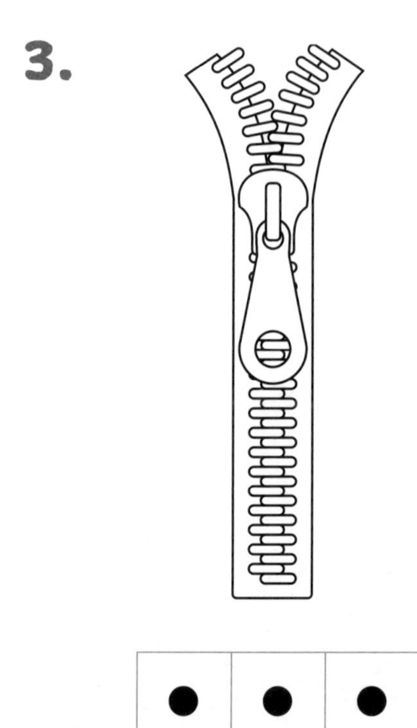

2.

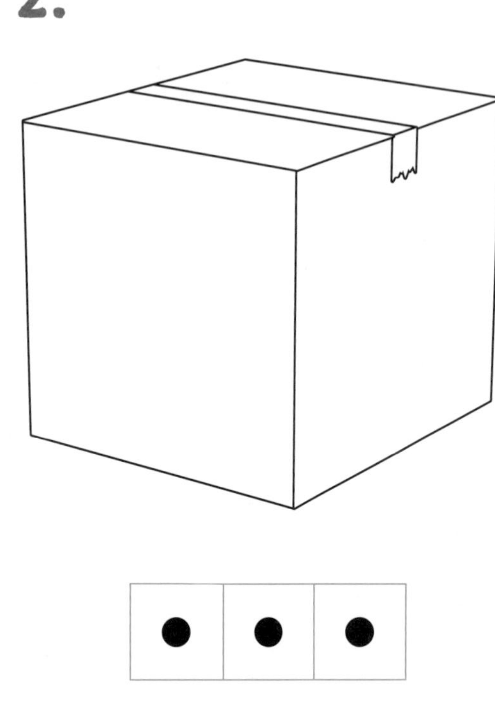

4.

Directions: Listen as I say the sounds for the first picture. *(Say the sounds for the first picture: /f/ /ĭ/ /x/.)* Touch the dot in each box as I repeat each sound in the word. *(Repeat the sounds /f/ /ĭ/ /x/.)* Run your finger across the boxes as we say the sounds together. What word is this? *(Repeat this process for all the pictures:* box, zip, *and* zoom.*)* Then, color the pictures.

Name: ______________________

1.

○ ○ ○

3.

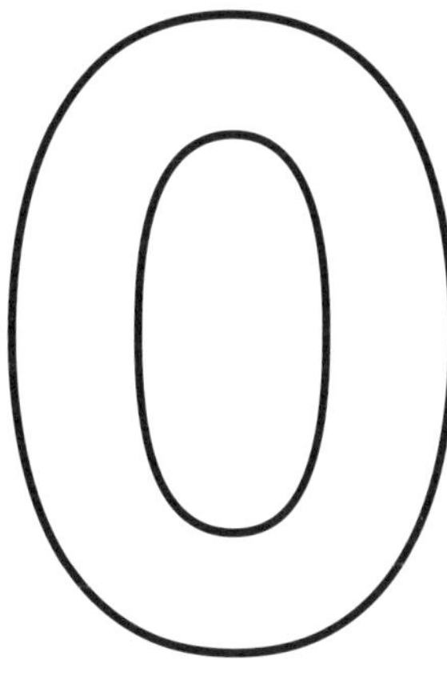

○ ○ ○ ○

2.

○ ○ ○

4.

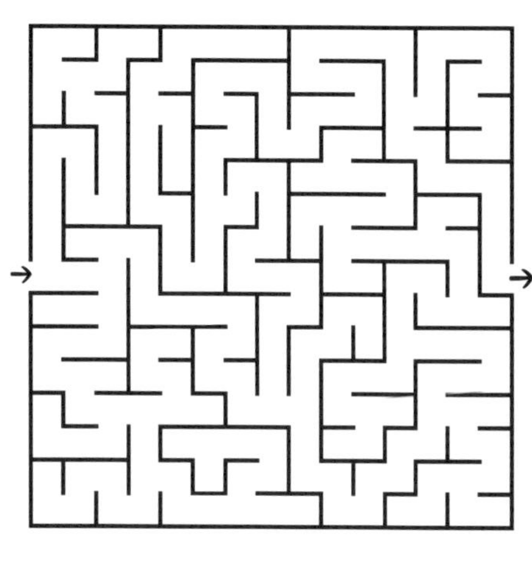

Directions: Listen as I say the word and each sound in the word for the first picture. *(Say the word* mix. *Then, say it slowly, stretching out each sound: /m/ /ĭ/ /x/.)* Touch the dot in each box as you say each sound in the word. Say the word again. This time, color the dots as you repeat the sounds in each word. *(Repeat this process for all the pictures.)* Then, color the pictures.

Name: ______________________

Directions: Trace the letters *E* and *e* with your finger while saying the sound /ĕ/. Name each picture. Say the first sound you hear in each word. Color the pictures that begin with the /ĕ/ sound. Write an *X* on the pictures that do not.

Name: ____________________

Directions: Trace the letters *Q* and *q* with your finger while saying the sound /qu/. Name each picture. Say the first sound you hear in each word. Color the pictures that begin with the /qu/ sound. Draw a line connecting each picture that begins with the /qu/ sound to the letters *Q* and *q*.

Name: ____________________

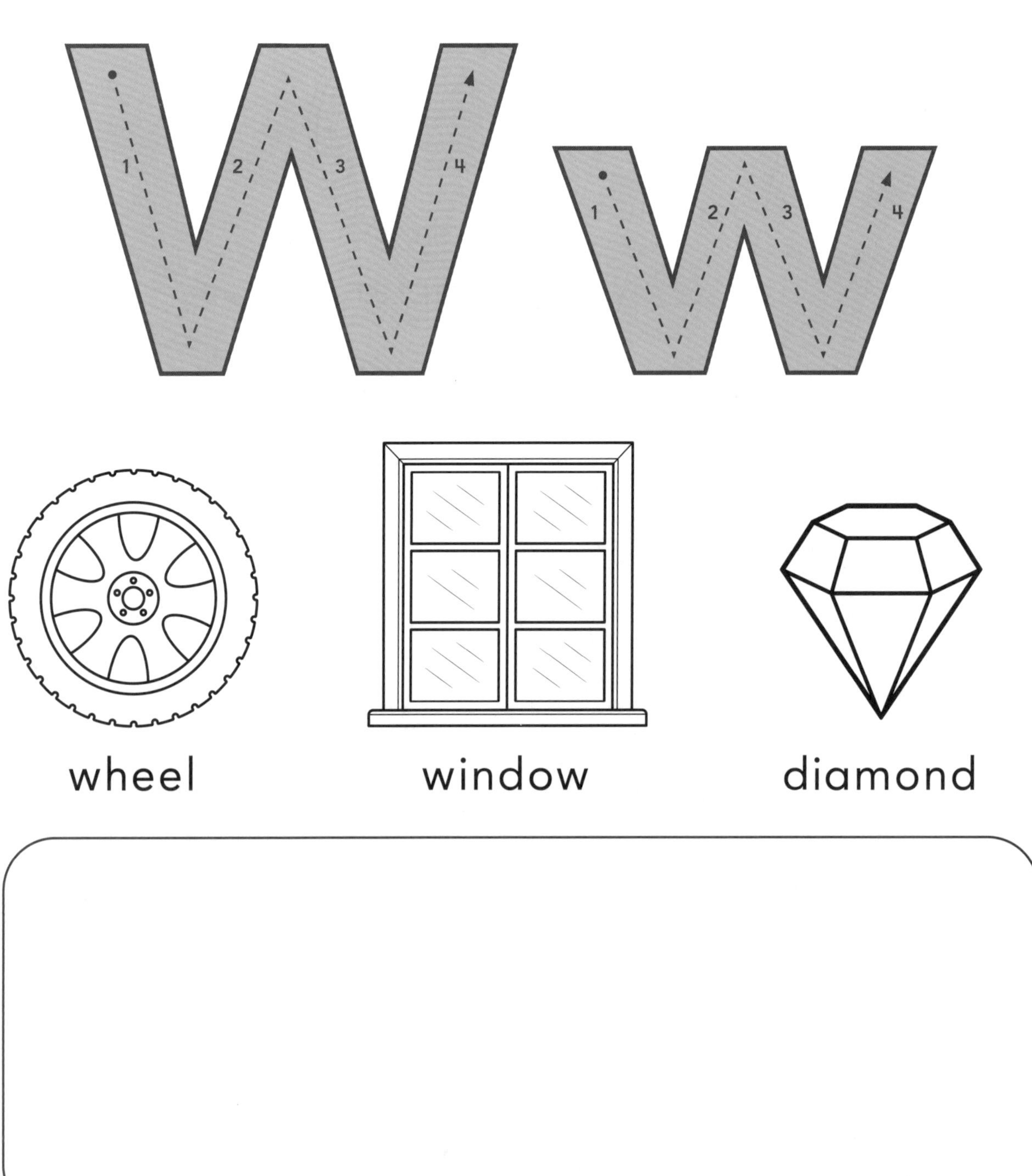

Directions: Trace the letters *W* and *w* with your finger while saying the sound /w/. Name each picture. Say the first sound you hear in each word. Color the pictures that begin with the /w/ sound. Draw two items that begin with the /w/ sound in the box.

Try This!

Write or draw an alphabet book or poster. Try to include at least one picture for each letter you have learned.

Name: ___________________________

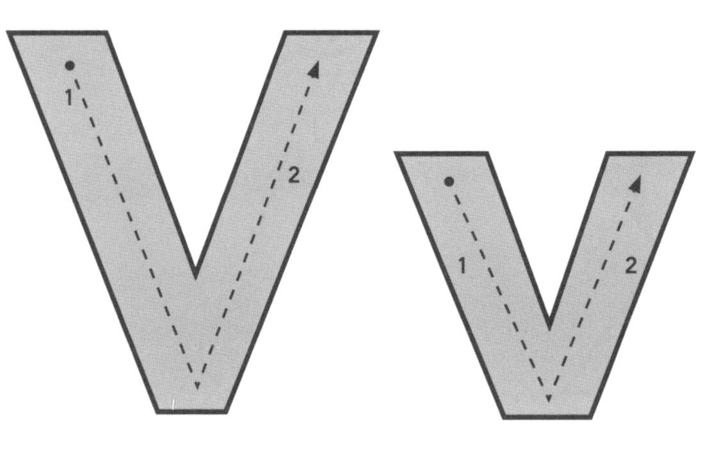

2.

●	●	●

1.

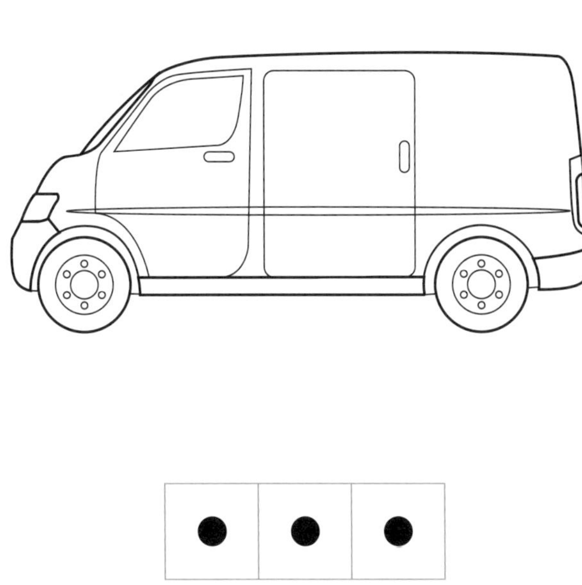

●	●	●

3.

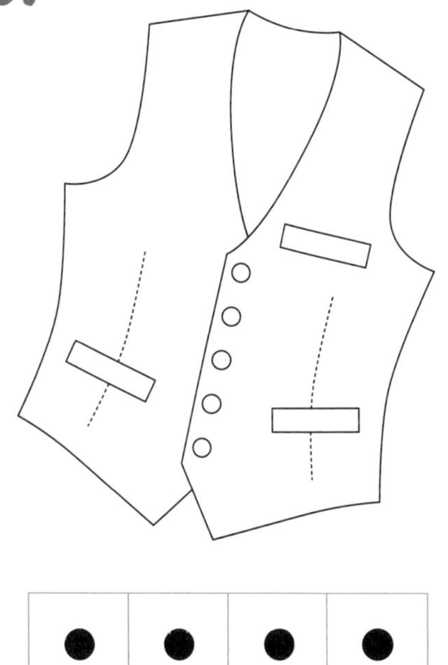

●	●	●	●

Directions: Trace the letters *V* and *v* with your finger while saying the sound /v/. Listen as I say the sounds for the first picture. *(Say the sounds for the first picture: /v/ /ă/ /n/.)* Touch the dot in each box as I repeat each sound in the word. *(Repeat the sounds /v/ /ă/ /n/.)* Run your finger across the boxes as we say the sounds together. What word is this? *(Repeat this process for all the pictures.)* Then, color the pictures.

Name: ______________________

Review: Ee, Qq, Ww, Vv, Xx, Zz

1\.

2\.

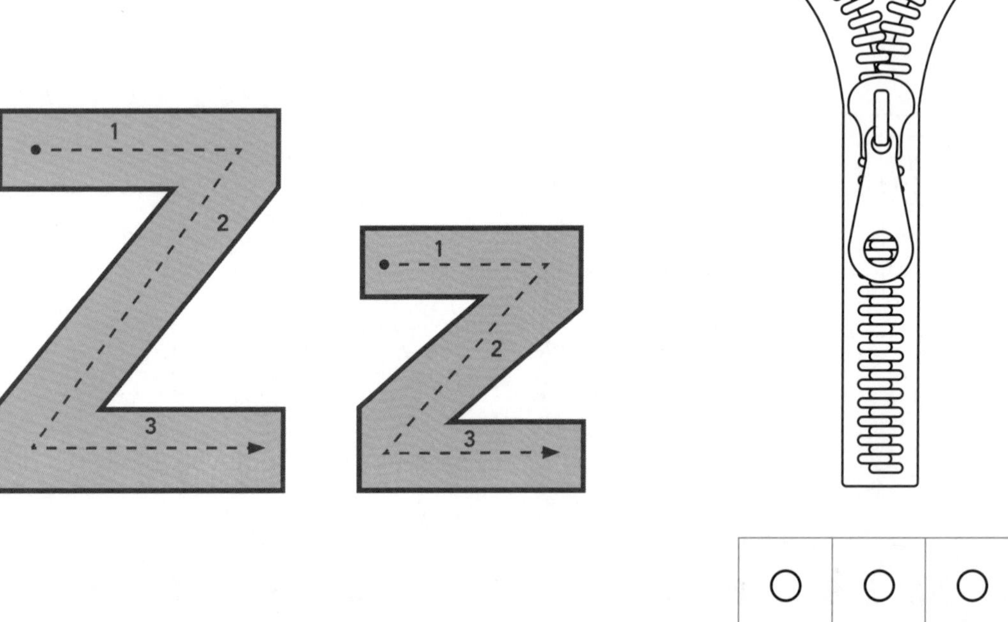

Directions: Trace the letters *X* and *x* with your finger while saying the sound /x/. Listen as I say the word and each sound in the word for the first picture. *(Say the word* fox. *Then, say it slowly, stretching out each sound: /f/ /ŏ/ /x/.)* Touch the dot in each box as you say each sound in the word. Say the word again. This time, color the dots as you repeat the sounds in the word. *(Repeat this process for the letters Z and z.)* Then, color the pictures.

Overview

Cumulative Review: Making CVC Words

Reading CVC words is a building block of early phonics instruction. CVC words consist of a consonant followed by a short vowel and then end with another consonant sound. In this unit, students will practice reading and writing CVC words. This is a great way for students to pull all their phonics knowledge together. It can also be rewarding for students as they begin to read and write whole words.

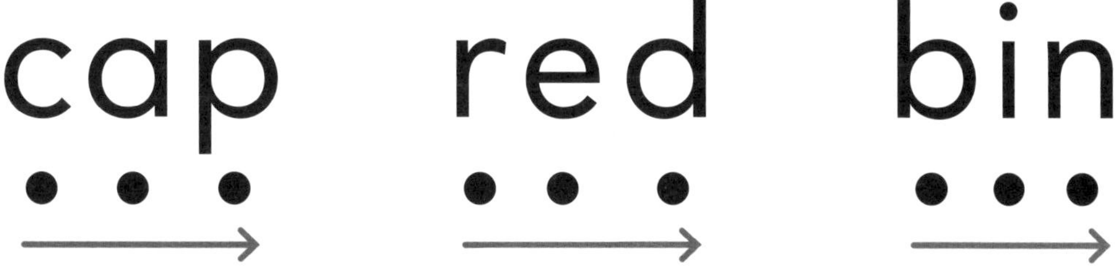

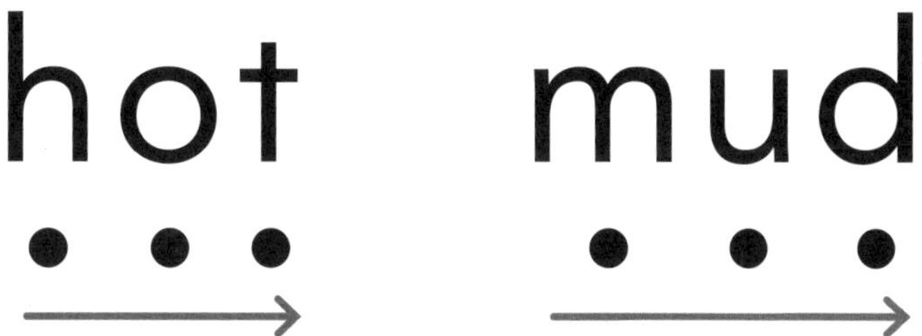

Directions: Look at the words. Blend the sounds to read each word. *(Run your finger under the letters from left to right, saying one sound for each letter, and then blending smoothly: /c/ /a/ /p/,* cap. *Repeat this process for the rest of the words.)*

Name: ______________________

CVC Words

net

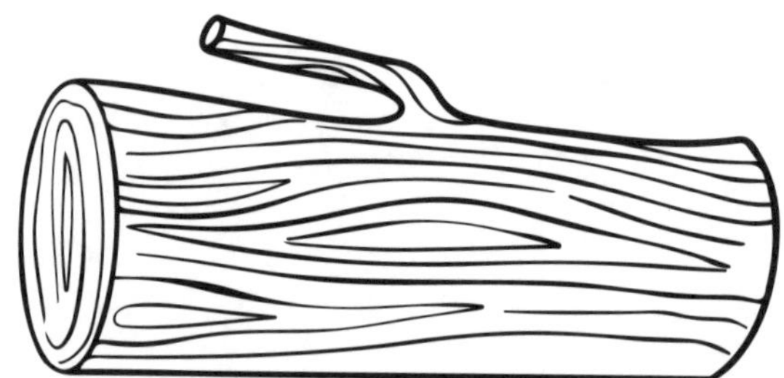

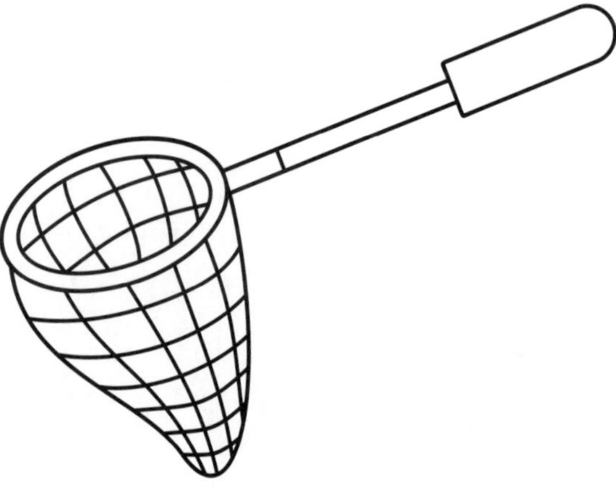

Directions: Touch the dots under each word. *(Say each sound as the student touches each dot.)* Run your finger under the letters while blending the sounds together. Then, say the word naturally. Draw a line from the word to the picture that matches. Then, color the pictures.

Name: ______________________

1.

	e	b

2.

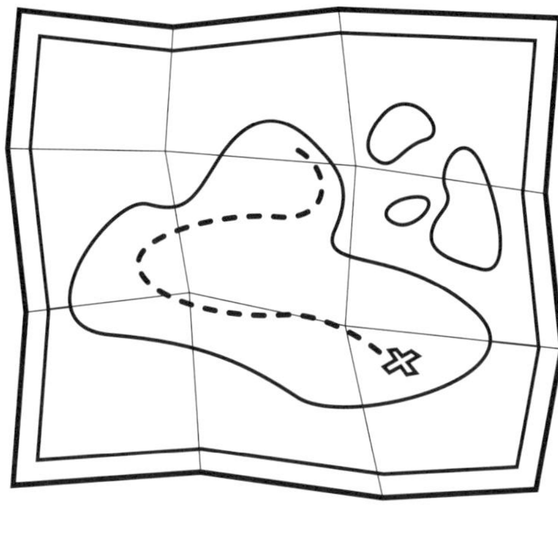

	a	p

3.

	a	d

4.

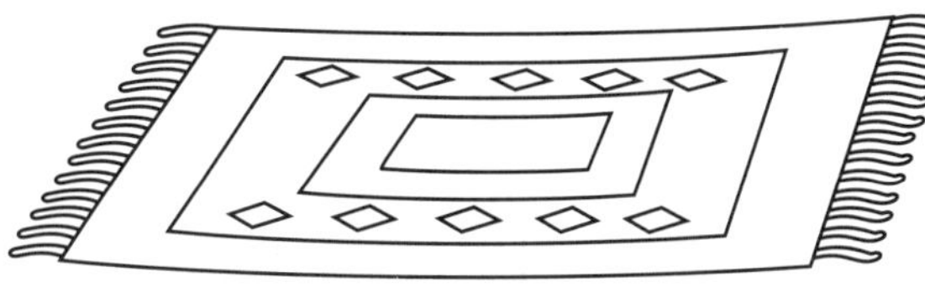

	u	g

CVC Words

Directions: Listen as I say the sounds for the first picture. *(Say the sounds for the first picture: /w/ /ĕ/ /b/.)* Run your finger across the boxes as we blend the sounds together. Say the first sound you hear in the word. Write the missing letter in the first box. *(Repeat this process for all the pictures.)* Then, color the pictures.

Name: ______________________

CVC Words

1.

r	a	

3.

l	e	

2.

f	a	

4.

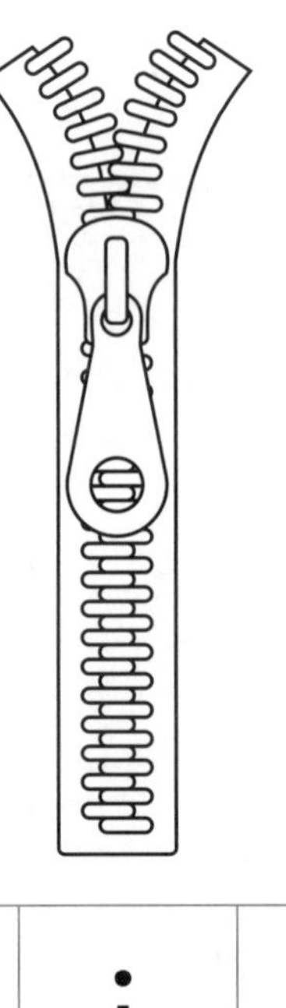

z	i	

Directions: Listen as I say the sounds for the first picture. *(Say the sounds for the first picture: /r/ /ă/ /t/.)* Run your finger across the boxes as we blend the sounds together. Say the final sound you hear in the word. Write the missing letter in the last box. *(Repeat this process for all the pictures.)* Then, color the pictures.

Name:

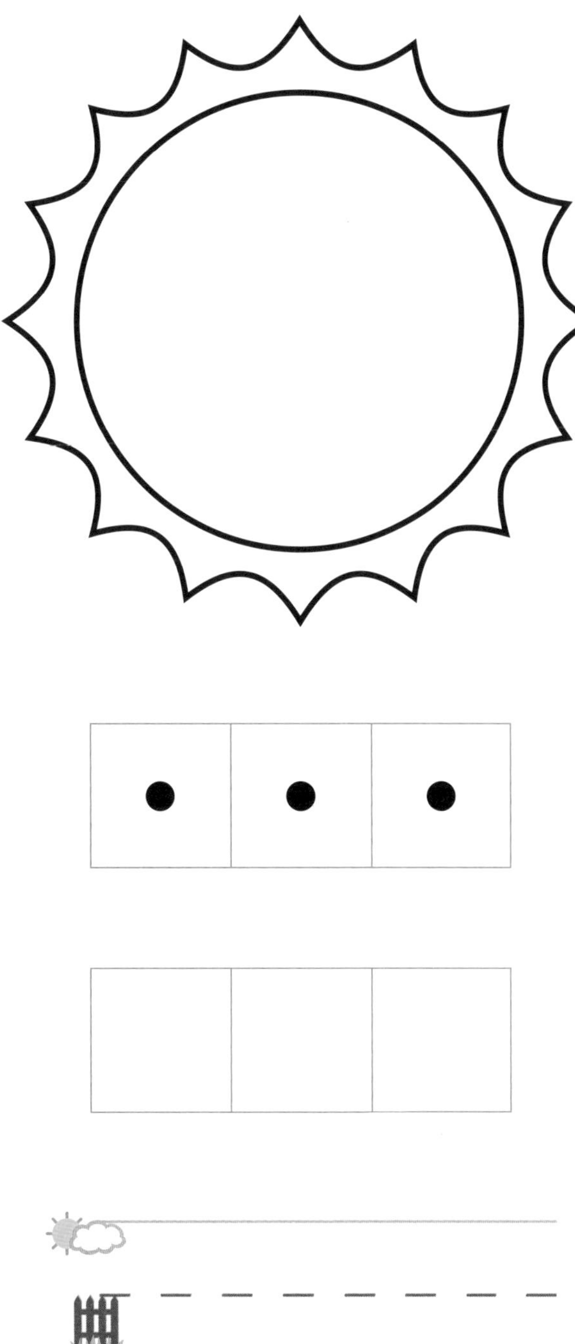

Directions: Name the picture. Listen as I say the sounds for the picture. *(Say the sounds /s/ /ŭ/ /n/.)* Touch the dot in each box as I repeat each sound in the word. *(Repeat the sounds /s/ /ŭ/ /n/.)* Run your finger across the boxes as we blend the sounds together. What sounds do you hear? Write the letters for each sound in the boxes. Write the whole word on the line. Then, color the picture.

Name: ______________________

1.

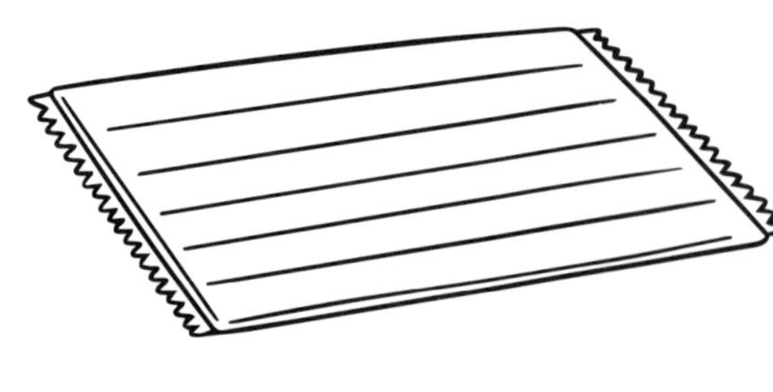

2.

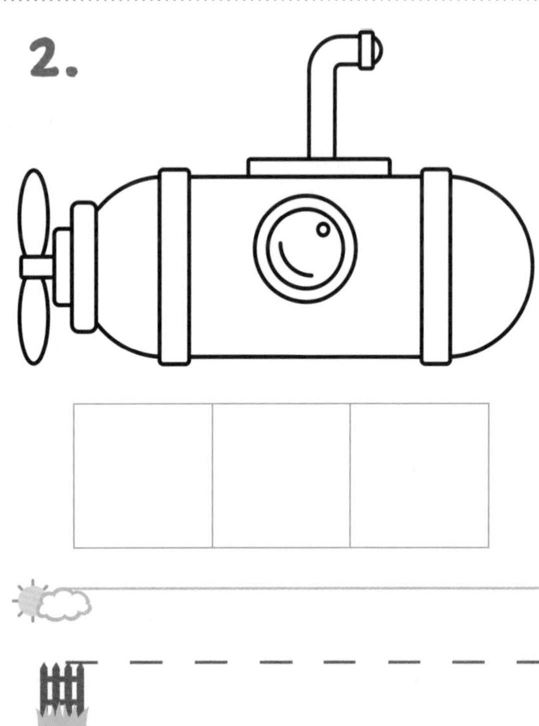

3.

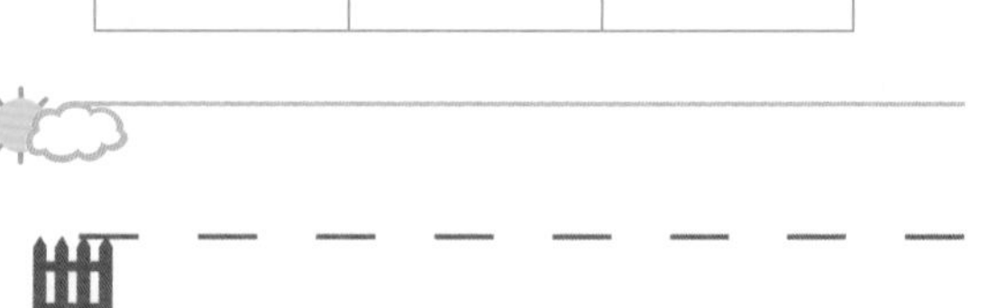

4.

Directions: Name the picture. Listen as I say the sounds for the picture. *(Say the sounds for the first picture: /m/ /ă/ /t/.)* Run your finger across the boxes as we blend the sounds together. What sounds do you hear? Write the letters for each sound you hear in the boxes. Write the whole word on the line. *(Repeat this process for all the pictures.)* Then, color the pictures.

Name: ______________________

cat

bag

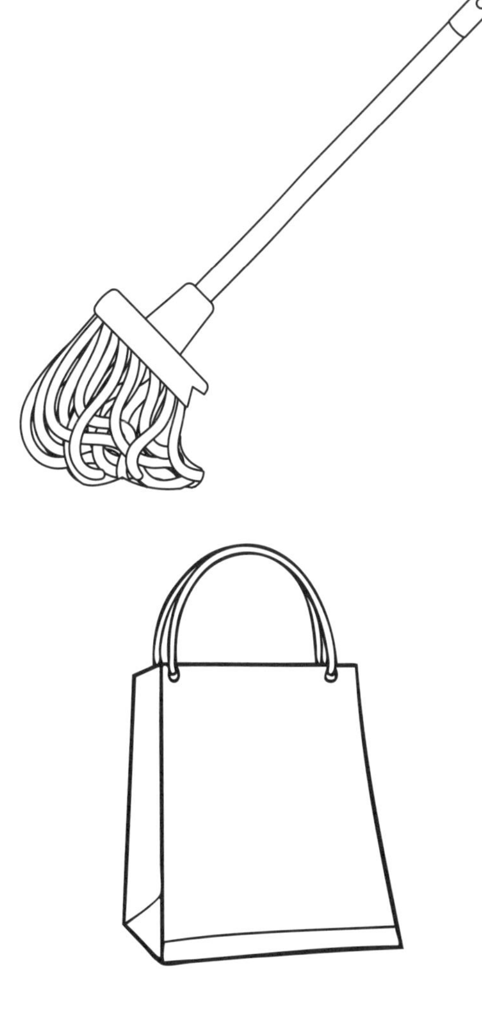

mop

Directions: Touch the dots under each word. *(Say each sound as the student touches each dot.)* Run your finger under the letters while blending the sounds together. Then, say the word naturally. Draw a line from the word to the picture that matches. Then, color the pictures.

Name: ____________________

1.

	o	t

2.

	a	p

3.

	o	m

4.

	a	t

Directions: Listen as I say the sounds for the first picture. *(Say the sounds for the first picture: /p/ /o/ /t/.)* Run your finger across the boxes as we say the sounds together. Say the first sound you hear in the word. Write the missing letter in the first box. *(Repeat this process for all the pictures.)* Then, color the pictures.

Name: ____________________

CVC Words

1.

p	a	

2.

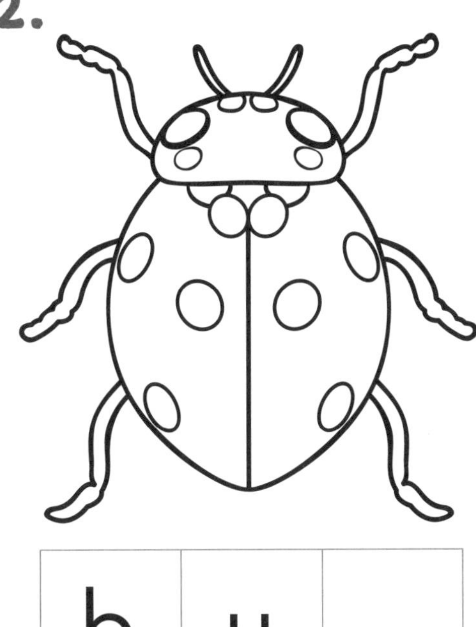

b	u	

3.

f	o	

4.

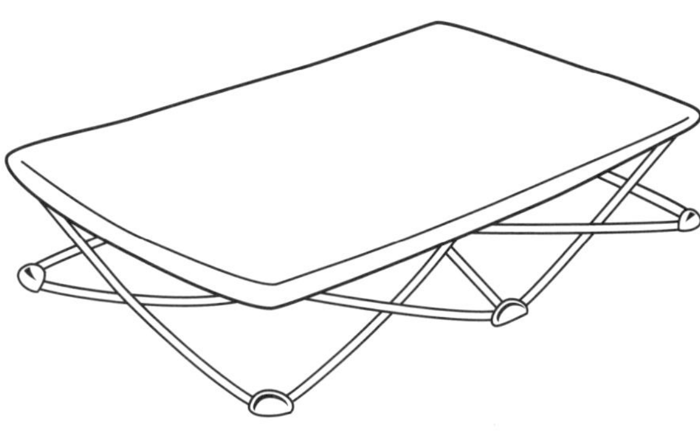

c	o	

Directions: Listen as I say the sounds for the first picture. *(Say the sounds for the first picture: /p/ /ă/ /n/.)* Run your finger across the boxes as we blend the sounds together. Say the final sound you hear in the word. Write the missing letter in the last box. *(Repeat this process for all the pictures.)* Then, color the pictures.

Name: ______________________

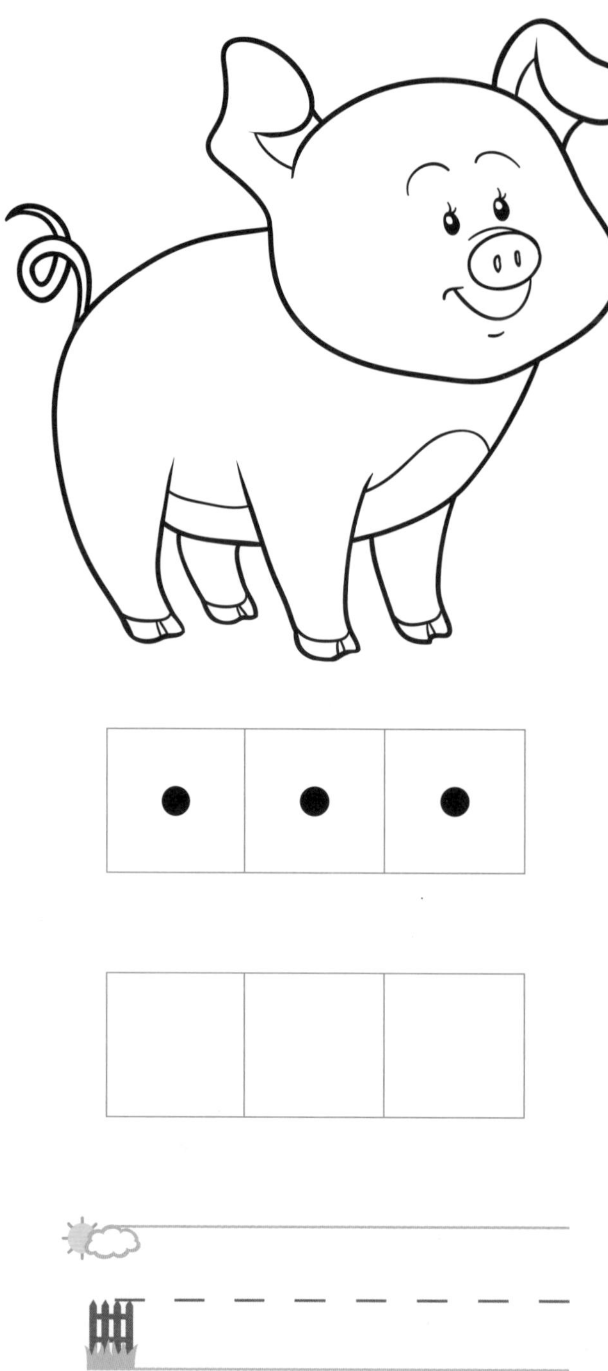

CVC Words

Directions: Name the picture. Listen as I say the sounds for the picture. *(Say the sounds /p/ /ĭ/ /g/.)* Touch the dot in each box as I repeat each sound in the word. *(Repeat the sounds /p/ /ĭ/ /g/.)* Run your finger across the boxes as we blend the sounds together. What sounds do you hear? Write the letters for each sound in the boxes. Write the whole word on the line. Then, color the picture.

Name: ____________________

1.

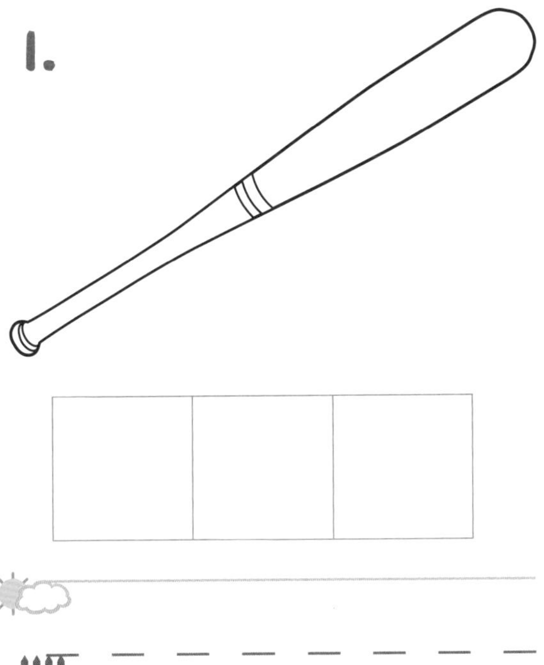

3.

2.

4.

Directions: Name the picture. Listen as I say the sounds for the picture. *(Say the sounds for the first picture: /b/ /ă/ /t/.)* Run your finger across the boxes as we blend the sounds together. What sounds do you hear? Write the letters for each sound you hear in the boxes. Write the whole word on the line. *(Repeat this process for all the pictures.)* Then, color the pictures.

Standards Correlations

Shell Education is committed to producing educational materials that are research and standards based. To support this effort, this resource is correlated to the academic standards of all 50 states, the District of Columbia, the Department of Defense Dependent Schools, and the Canadian provinces. A correlation is also provided for key professional educational organizations.

To print a customized correlation report for your state, visit our website at **www.tcmpub.com/administrators/correlations** and follow the online directions. If you require assistance in printing correlation reports, please contact the Customer Service Department at 1-800-858-7339.

Standards Overview

The Every Student Succeeds Act (ESSA) mandates that all states adopt challenging academic standards that help students meet the goal of college and career readiness. While many states already adopted academic standards prior to ESSA, the act continues to hold states accountable for detailed and comprehensive standards. Standards are designed to focus instruction and guide adoption of curricula. They define the knowledge, skills, and content students should acquire at each level. Standards are also used to develop standardized tests to evaluate students' academic progress. State standards are used in the development of our resources, so educators can be assured they meet state academic requirements.

College and Career Readiness

Today's college and career readiness (CCR) standards offer guidelines for preparing K–12 students with the knowledge and skills that are necessary to succeed in postsecondary job training and education. CCR standards include the Common Core State Standards as well as other state-adopted standards such as the Texas Essential Knowledge and Skills. The standards found on page 199 describe the content presented throughout the lessons.

TESOL and WIDA Standards

English language development standards are integrated within each lesson to enable English learners to work toward proficiency in English while learning content—developing the skills and confidence in listening, speaking, reading, and writing. The standards found in the digital resources describe the language objectives presented throughout the lessons.

Standards Correlations (cont.)

180 Days™: Phonics for Prekindergarten offers a full page of daily phonics practice activities for each day of the school year. Every week provides practice activities tied to a variety of language arts standards, providing students the opportunity for regular practice in decoding, word recognition, phonics, reading, and writing.

Reading Foundation Skills

Print Concepts
Recognize and name all uppercase and lowercase letters of the alphabet.
Demonstrate understanding of the organization and basic features of print.
Follow words from left to right and top to bottom.
Recognize that spoken words are represented in written language by specific sequences of letters.
Phonological Awareness
Demonstrate understanding of spoken words, syllables, and sounds (phonemes).
Count, pronounce, blend, and segment syllables in spoken words.
Blend and segment onsets and rimes of spoken words.
Phonics and Word Recognition
Know and apply grade-level phonics and word-analysis skills in decoding words.
Demonstrate basic knowledge of one-to-one letter-sound correspondences by producing the primary sound or many of the most frequent sounds for each consonant.
Associate the short sounds with common spellings (graphemes) for the five major vowels.

References Cited

Beck, Isabel L., and Mark E. Beck, 2013. *Making Sense of Phonics: The Hows and Whys, Second Edition*. New York: Guilford.

Marzano, Robert, 2010. "When Practice Makes Perfect Sense." *Educational Leadership* 68 (3): 81–83.

National Reading Panel, 2000. *Report of the National Reading Panel: Teaching Children to Read*. Report of the Subgroups. Washington, DC: U.S. Department of Health and Human Services, National Institutes of Health.

Answer Key

There are several open-ended prompts in this book. For those activities, answers will vary, and example answers are provided when possible.

Unit 1

Week 1

Day 1 (page 12)

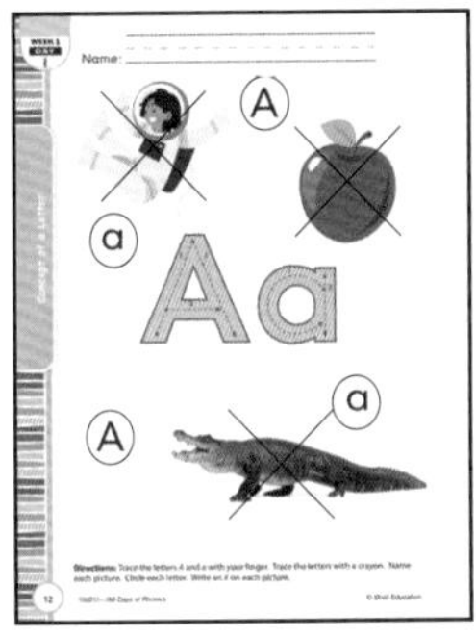

Day 2 (page 13)

Day 3 (page 14)

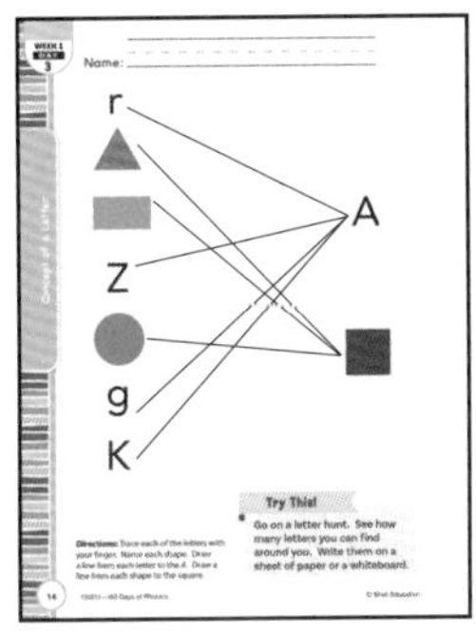

Day 4 (page 15)

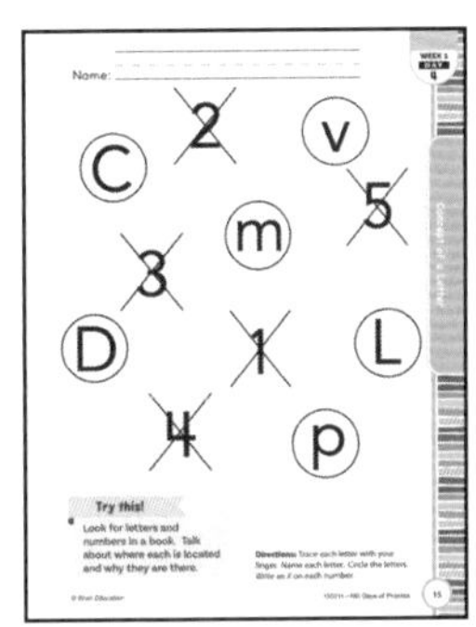

Day 5 (page 16)

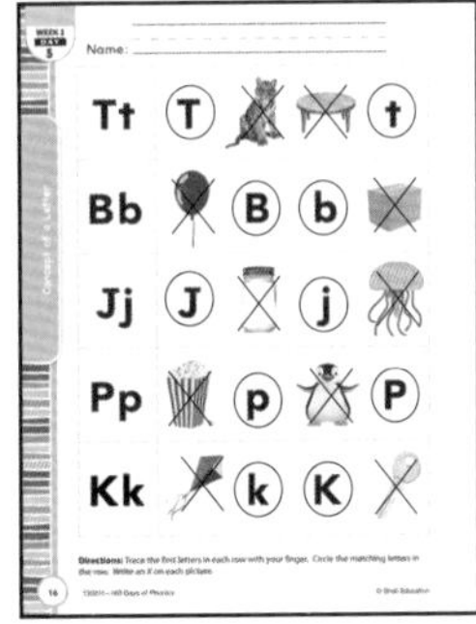

Week 2

Day 1 (page 17)

Students should color the *c* and *e* in different colors.

Day 2 (page 18)

Students should circle the first letter and underline the last letter in their names.

Day 3 (page 19)

hat
tie
boot
sock

Answer Key (cont.)

Day 4 (page 20)

log
leaf
tree
acorn

Day 5 (page 21)

dog
fish
bird
cat
horse
frog

Week 3

Day 1 (page 22)

The pictures are *broccoli, carrot, pumpkin,* and *corn*.

Day 2 (page 23)

Row 1: pencil, glue, book
Row 2: scissors, crayon, backpack
Row 3: paper, paintbrush, blocks

Day 3 (page 24)

Row 1: circle, triangle, square
Row 2: rectangle, heart, star
Row 3: oval, rectangle, rhombus/diamond

Day 4 (page 25)

Look for students moving their fingers as you read the letters.

Day 5 (page 26)

Look for students moving their fingers as you read the text.

Week 4

Day 1 (page 27)

Look for students matching their drawings to the labels.

Day 2 (page 28)

Day 3 (page 29)

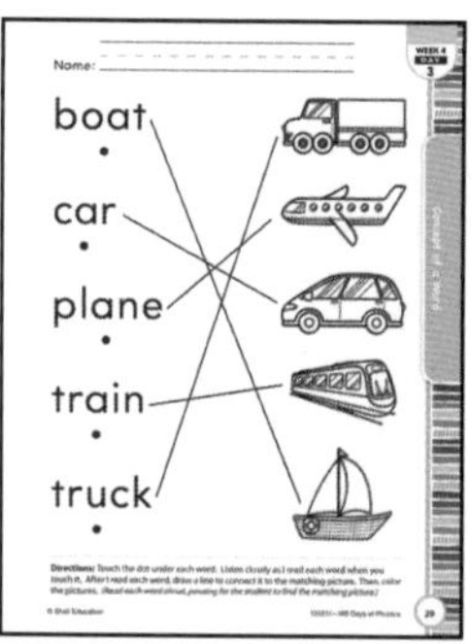

Day 4 (page 30)

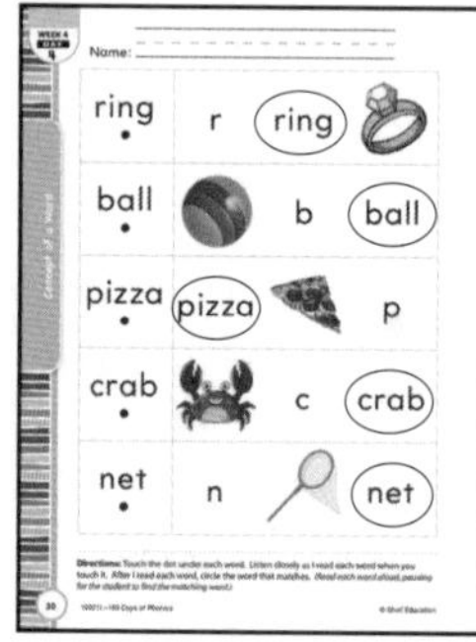

Day 5 (page 31)

Students should trace the number 4 and draw a line from the number 4 to the sentence.

Answer Key (cont.)

Unit 2

Week 5

Day 1 (page 33)

Listen for students identifying the /ă/ sound.

Day 2 (page 34)

The pictures are *table*, *man*, *apple*, and *spoon*. Students should circle *apple*.

Day 3 (page 35)

The first set of pictures are *goat*, *astronaut*, *pear*, and *kite*. Students should circle *astronaut*.

The second set of pictures are *alligator*, *nest*, and *eggs*. Students should color *alligator*.

Day 4 (page 36)

1. apple ap-ple
2. ambulance am-bu-lance
3. astronaut as-tro-naut
4. arrow ar-row

Day 5 (page 37)

1. acrobat ac-ro-bat
2. antlers ant-lers
3. alligator al-li-ga-tor
4. avocado av-o-ca-do

Week 6

Day 1 (page 38)

Listen for students identifying the /m/ sound.

Day 2 (page 39)

The pictures are *snake*, *mitten*, *alligator*, and *tomato*. Students should circle *mitten*.

Day 3 (page 40)

The first set of pictures are *mushroom*, *avocado*, *sunglasses*, and *tent*. Students should circle *mushroom*.

The second set of pictures are *monkey*, *moon*, and *pencil*. Students should color *monkey* and *moon*.

Day 4 (page 41)

1. man /m/ /an/
2. mat /m/ /at/
3. mop /m/ /op/
4. moon /m/ /oon/

Day 5 (page 42)

1. mad /m/ /ad/
2. mud /m/ /ud/
3. mug /m/ /ug/
4. mom /m/ /om/

Week 7

Day 1 (page 43)

Listen for students identifying the /t/ sound.

Day 2 (page 44)

The pictures are *snowflake*, *axe*, *mouth*, and *tiger*. Students should circle *tiger*.

Day 3 (page 45)

The first set of pictures are *foot*, *bread*, *treasure*, and *watch*. Students should circle *treasure*.

The second set of pictures are *pie*, *ticket*, and *tree*. Students should color *ticket* and *tree*.

Day 4 (page 46)

1. top /t/ /ŏ/ /p/
2. ten /t/ /ĕ/ /n/
3. tail /t/ /ā/ /l/
4. tape /t/ /ā/ /p/

Day 5 (page 47)

1. tug /t/ /ŭ/ /g/
2. tack /t/ /ă/ /ck/
3. tag /t/ /ă/ /g/
4. tube /t/ /ū/ /b/

Week 8

Day 1 (page 48)

Listen for students identifying the /s/ sound.

Day 2 (page 49)

The pictures are *soup*, *mitten*, *net*, and *cup*. Students should circle *soup*.

Day 3 (page 50)

The first set of pictures are *moon*, *grass*, *cloud*, and *spoon*. Students should circle *spoon*.

The second set of pictures are *star*, *jacket*, and *seal*. Students should color *star* and *seal*.

Answer Key (cont.)

Day 4 (page 51)

1. sit /s/ /it/
2. seed /s/ /eed/
3. salt /s/ /alt/
4. sad /s/ /ad/

Day 5 (page 52)

1. sun /s/ /un/
2. sub /s/ /ub/
3. soap /s/ /oap/
4. sock /s/ /ock/

Week 9

Day 1 (page 53)

Listen for students identifying the /p/ sound.

Day 2 (page 54)

The pictures are *milk*, *puzzle*, *scissors*, and *apple*. Students should circle *puzzle*.

Day 3 (page 55)

The first set of pictures are *piano*, *suitcase*, *moon*, and *ax*. Students should circle *piano*.

The second set of pictures are *trumpet*, *penguin*, and *peanut*. Students should color *penguin* and *peanut*.

Day 4 (page 56)

1. pig /p/ /ĭ/ /g/
2. pan /p/ /ă/ /n/
3. map /m/ /ă/ /p/
4. cap /c/ /ă/ /p/

Day 5 (page 57)

1. pen /p/ /ĕ/ /n/
2. pot /p/ /ŏ/ /t/
3. pup /p/ /ŭ/ /p/
4. hop /h/ /ŏ/ /p/

Week 10

Day 1 (page 58)

Day 2 (page 59)

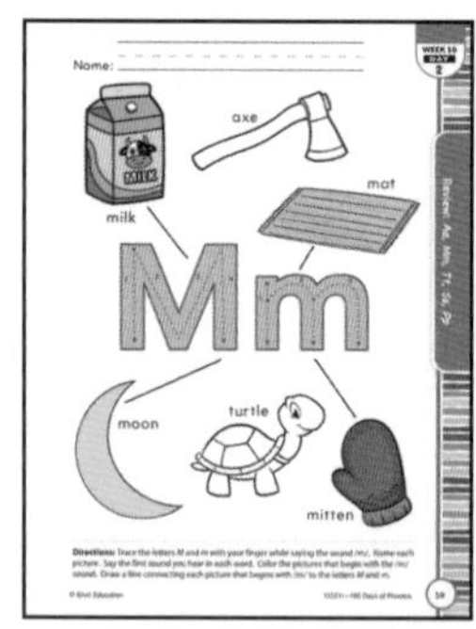

Day 3 (page 60)

Students should color *top* and *tent*.

Day 4 (page 61)

1. sun /s/ /ŭ/ /n/
2. sub /s/ /ŭ/ /b/
3. sad /s/ /ă/ /d/

Day 5 (page 62)

1. pup /p/ /ŭ/ /p/
2. pot /p/ /ŏ/ /t/
3. pig /p/ /ĭ/ /g/

Answer Key (cont.)

Unit 3

Week 11

Day 1 (page 64)

Listen for students identifying the /ĭ/ sound.

Day 2 (page 65)

The pictures are *flag*, *ball*, *igloo*, and *glue*. Students should circle *igloo*.

Day 3 (page 66)

The first set of pictures are *plane*, *star*, *table*, and *iguana*. Students should circle *iguana*.

The second set of pictures are *insect*, *turtle*, and *paintbrush*. Students should color *insect*.

Day 4 (page 67)

1. inside in-side
2. infant in-fant
3. iguana i-gua-na
4. instrument in-stru-ment

Day 5 (page 68)

1. insect in-sect
2. igloo ig-loo
3. into in-to
4. invitation in-vi-ta-tion

Week 12

Day 1 (page 69)

Listen for students identifying the /n/ sound.

Day 2 (page 70)

The pictures are *peach*, *dog*, *spoon*, and *nut*. Students should circle *nut*.

Day 3 (page 71)

The first set of pictures are *nail*, *slide*, *moth*, and *taco*. Students should circle *newspaper*.

The second set of pictures are *igloo*, *nest*, and *pillow*. Students should color *nest*.

Day 4 (page 72)

1. nut /n/ /ut/
2. nose /n/ /ose/
3. nail /n/ /ail/
4. nest /n/ /est/

Day 5 (page 73)

1. net /n/ /et/
2. note /n/ /ote/
3. neck /n/ /eck/
4. noon /n/ /oon/

Week 13

Day 1 (page 74)

Listen for students identifying the /f/ sound.

Day 2 (page 75)

The pictures are *flag*, *pajamas*, *necklace*, and *cat*. Students should circle *flag*.

Day 3 (page 76)

The first set of pictures are *strawberry*, *pants*, *map*, and *foot*. Students should circle *foot*.

The second set of pictures are *frog*, *rug*, and *fire*. Students should color *frog* and *fire*.

Day 4 (page 77)

1. fan /f/ /ă/ /n/
2. fin /f/ /ĭ/ /n/
3. fish /f/ /ĭ/ /sh/
4. foot /f/ /o͝o/ /t/

Day 5 (page 78)

1. food /f/ /o͞o/ /d/
2. fig /f/ /ĭ/ /g/
3. fox /f/ /ŏ/ /x/
4. frog /f/ /r/ /ŏ/ /g/

Week 14

Day 1 (page 79)

Listen for students identifying the /g/ sound.

Day 2 (page 80)

The pictures are *pencil*, *notebook*, *mop*, and *game*. Students should circle *game*.

Day 3 (page 81)

The first set of pictures are *astronaut*, *tooth*, *plant*, and *goose*. Students should circle *goose*.

The second set of pictures are *bat*, *glue*, and *grapes*. Students should color *glue* and *grapes*.

Answer Key (cont.)

Day 4 (page 82)

1. goat /g/ /oat/
2. golf /g/ /olf/
3. girl /g/ /irl/
4. game /g/ /ame/

Day 5 (page 83)

1. ghost /gh/ /ost/
2. gum /g/ /um/
3. gate /g/ /ate/
4. goose /g/ /oose/

Week 15

Day 1 (page 84)

Listen for students identifying the /b/ sound.

Day 2 (page 85)

The pictures are *bed*, *paint*, *mug*, and *nose*. Students should circle *bed*.

Day 3 (page 86)

The first set of pictures are *tree*, *flower*, *broccoli*, and *gift*. Students should circle *broccoli*.

The second set of pictures are *brush*, *book*, and *lamp*. Students should color *brush* and *book*.

Day 4 (page 87)

1. bus /b/ /ŭ/ /s/
2. bag /b/ /ă/ /g/
3. bat /b/ /ă/ /t/
4. cab /c/ /ă/ /b/

Day 5 (page 88)

1. bed /b/ /ĕ/ /d/
2. bib /b/ /ĭ/ /b/
3. bin /b/ /ĭ/ /n/
4. sub /s/ /ŭ/ /b/

Week 16

Day 1 (page 89)

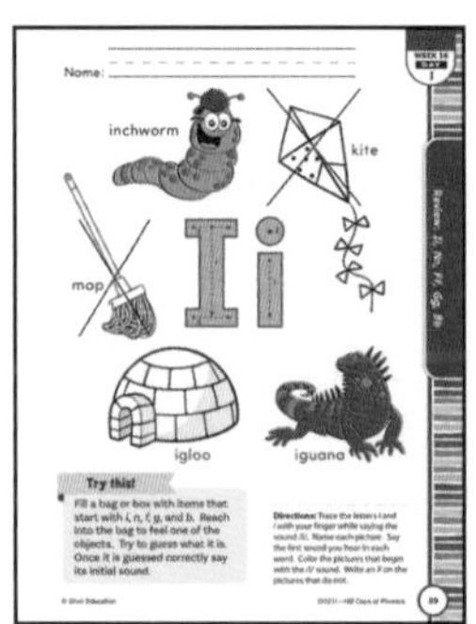

Day 2 (page 90)

Day 3 (page 91)

Students should color *flower* and *fan*.

Day 4 (page 92)

1. gap /g/ /ă/ /p/
2. gum /g/ /ŭ/ /m/
3. gas /g/ /ă/ /s/

Day 5 (page 93)

1. bun /b/ /ŭ/ /n/
2. bag /b/ /ă/ /g/
3. bat /b/ /ă/ /t/

Answer Key (cont.)

Unit 4

Week 17

Day 1 (page 95)

Listen for students identifying the /ŏ/ sound.

Day 2 (page 96)

The pictures are *bubbles*, *goat*, *ostrich*, and *net*. Students should circle *ostrich*.

Day 3 (page 97)

The first set of pictures are *pumpkin*, *mat*, *octopus*, and *soup*. Students should circle *octopus*.

The second set of pictures are *butterfly*, *otter*, and *fish*. Students should color *otter*.

Day 4 (page 98)

1. cot /c/ /ŏ/ /t/
2. dog /d/ /ŏ/ /g/
3. mop /m/ /ŏ/ /p/
4. sock /s/ /ŏ/ /ck/

Day 5 (page 99)

1. pot /p/ /ŏ/ /t/
2. log /l/ /ŏ/ /g/
3. lock /l/ /ŏ/ /ck/
4. hop /h/ /ŏ/ /p/

Week 18

Day 1 (page 100)

Listen for students identifying the /c/ sound.

Day 2 (page 101)

The pictures are *man*, *cookie*, *bug*, and *pool*. Students should circle *cookie*.

Day 3 (page 102)

The first set of pictures are *castle*, *glasses*, *book*, and *insect*. Students should circle *castle*.

The second set of pictures are *fish*, *corn*, and *camel*. Students should color *corn* and *camel*.

Day 4 (page 103)

1. cup /c/ /up/
2. cat /c/ /at/
3. can /c/ /an/
4. candle /c/ /andle/

Day 5 (page 104)

1. car /c/ /ar/
2. cow /c/ /ow/
3. camel /c/ /amel/
4. cake /c/ /ake/

Week 19

Day 1 (page 105)

Listen for students identifying the /l/ sound.

Day 2 (page 106)

The pictures are *pizza*, *iguana*, *moose*, and *lamp*. Students should circle *lamp*.

Day 3 (page 107)

The first set of pictures are *fan*, *bread*, *caterpillar*, and *ladder*. Students should circle *ladder*.

The second set of pictures are *bird*, *log*, and *gate*. Students should color *log*.

Day 4 (page 108)

1. log /l/ /ŏ/ /g/
2. lock /l/ /ŏ/ /k/
3. ball /b/ /ă/ /l/
4. pool /p/ /ōō/ /l/

Day 5 (page 109)

1. leg /l/ /ĕ/ /g/
2. lime /l/ /ī/ /m/
3. hill /h/ /ĭ/ /l/
4. bell /b/ /ĕ/ /l/

Week 20

Day 1 (page 110)

Listen for students identifying the /h/ sound.

Day 2 (page 111)

The pictures are *coin*, *house*, *ticket*, and *plant*. Students should circle *house*.

Day 3 (page 112)

The first set of pictures are *hive*, *peas*, *flamingo*, and *grapes*. Students should circle *hive*.

The second set of pictures are *hand*, *fox*, and *bell*. Students should color *hand*.

Answer Key (cont.)

Day 4 (page 113)

1. hog /h/ /ŏ/ /g/
2. hat /h/ /ă/ /t/
3. hill /h/ /ĭ/ /l/
4. hand /h/ /ă/ /n/ /d/

Day 5 (page 114)

1. hen /h/ /ĕ/ /n/
2. hip /h/ /ĭ/ /p/
3. hop /h/ /ŏ/ /p/
4. hook /h/ /o͝o/ /k/

Week 21

Day 1 (page 115)

Listen for students identifying the /j/ sound.

Day 2 (page 116)

The pictures are *skirt*, *jam*, *ninja*, and *tiger*. Students should circle *jam*.

Day 3 (page 117)

The first set of pictures are *jump rope*, *penguin*, *corn*, and *farm*. Students should circle *jump rope*.

The second set of pictures are *jellyfish*, *broccoli*, and *log*. Students should color *jellyfish*.

Day 4 (page 118)

1. jet /j/ /ĕ/ /t/
2. jug /j/ /ŭ/ /g/
3. jam /j/ /ă/ /m/
4. jump /j/ /ŭ/ /m/ /p/

Day 5 (page 119)

1. June /j/ /ū/ /n/
2. jar /j/ /ar/
3. jog /j/ /ŏ/ /g/
4. juice /j/ /oo/ /s/

Week 22

Day 1 (page 120)

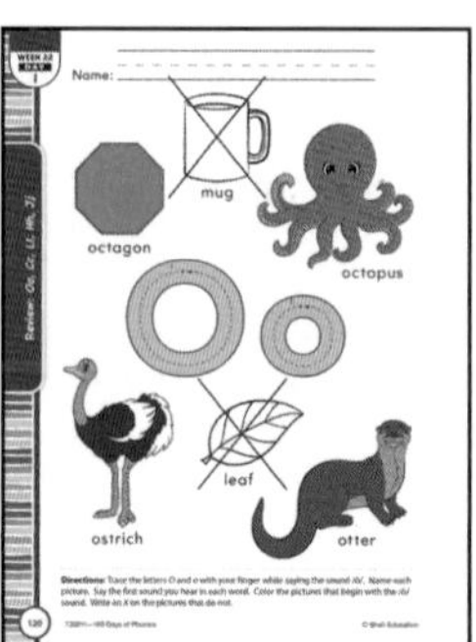

Day 2 (page 121)

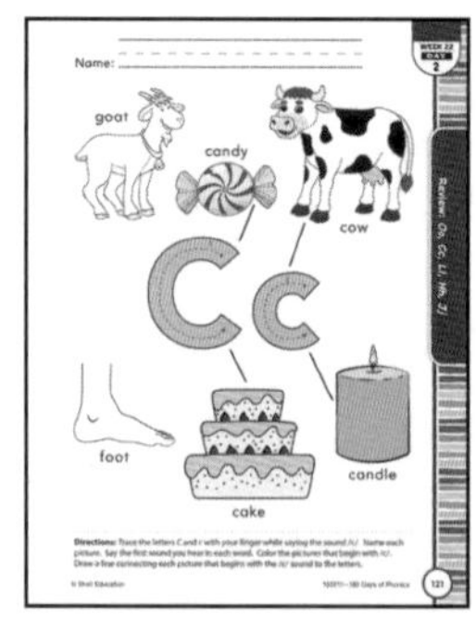

Day 3 (page 122)

Students should color *leaf* and *log*.

Day 4 (page 123)

1. hop /h/ /ŏ/ /p/
2. hen /h/ /ĕ/ /n/
3. hat /h/ /ă/ /t/

Day 5 (page 124)

1. jog /j/ /ŏ/ /g/
2. jam /j/ /ă/ /m/
3. jug /j/ /ŭ/ /g/

Answer Key (cont.)

Unit 5

Week 23

Day 1 (page 126)

Listen for students identifying the /ŭ/ sound.

Day 2 (page 127)

The pictures are *lemon*, *octopus*, *pasta*, and *umbrella*. Students should circle *umbrella*.

Day 3 (page 128)

The first set of pictures are *bow*, *upstairs*, *ghost*, and *frog*. Students should circle *upstairs*.

The second set of pictures are *umpire*, *bear*, and *candle*. Students should color *umpire*.

Day 4 (page 129)

1. gum /g/ /ŭ/ /m/
2. bug /b/ /ŭ/ /g/
3. bus /b/ /ŭ/ /s/
4. sun /s/ /ŭ/ /n/

Day 5 (page 130)

1. bun /b/ /ŭ/ /n/
2. mug /m/ /ŭ/ /g/
3. cub /c/ /ŭ/ /b/
4. nut /n/ /ŭ/ /t/

Week 24

Day 1 (page 131)

Listen for students identifying the /r/ sound.

Day 2 (page 132)

The pictures are *ring*, *treasure*, *pan*, and *nurse*. Students should circle *ring*.

Day 3 (page 133)

The first set of pictures are *foot*, *grass*, *rock*, and *banana*. Students should circle *rock*.

The second set of pictures are *rabbit*, *bed*, and *rose*. Students should color *rabbit* and *rose*.

Day 4 (page 134)

1. rug /r/ /ug/
2. rose /r/ /ose/
3. rat /r/ /at/
4. ram /r/ /am/

Day 5 (page 135)

1. rice /r/ /ice/
2. rope /r/ /ope/
3. ring /r/ /ing/
4. rake /r/ /ake/

Week 25

Day 1 (page 136)

Listen for students identifying the /k/ sound.

Day 2 (page 137)

The pictures are *moon*, *pig*, *kangaroo*, and *newspaper*. Students should circle *kangaroo*.

Day 3 (page 138)

The first set of pictures are *fence*, *glue*, *balloon*, and *king*. Students should circle *king*.

The second set of pictures are *bib*, *koala*, and *sun*. Students should color *koala*.

Day 4 (page 139)

1. kid /k/ /ĭ/ /d/
2. kite /k/ /ī/ /t/
3. kick /k/ /ĭ/ /k/
4. rake /r/ /ā/ /k/

Day 5 (page 140)

1. kit /k/ /ĭ/ /t/
2. key /k/ /ē/ /y/
3. duck /d/ /ŭ/ /k/
4. sock /s/ /ŏ/ /k/

Week 26

Day 1 (page 141)

Listen for students identifying the /d/ sound.

Day 2 (page 142)

The pictures are *pickle*, *gum*, *ball*, and *desk*. Students should circle *desk*.

Day 3 (page 143)

The first set of pictures are *doctor*, *fish*, *otter*, and *castle*. Students should circle *doctor*.

The second set of pictures are *domino*, *dollar*, and *lion*. Students should color *domino* and *dollar*.

Answer Key (cont.)

Day 4 (page 144)

1. dog /d/ /ŏ/ /g/
2. den /d/ /ĕ/ /n/
3. duck /d/ /ŭ/ /k/
4. bed /b/ /ĕ/ /d/

Day 5 (page 145)

1. dig /d/ /ĭ/ /g/
2. doll /d/ /ŏ/ /l/
3. mad /m/ /ă/ /d/
4. sad /s/ /ă/ /d/

Week 27

Day 1 (page 146)

Listen for students identifying the /y/ sound.

Day 2 (page 147)

The pictures are *turkey*, *yolk*, *pen*, and *game*. Students should circle *yolk*.

Day 3 (page 148)

The first set of pictures are *moon*, *lemon*, *yawn*, and *boat*. Students should circle *yawn*.

The second set of pictures are *foot*, *candy*, and *yoyo*. Students should color *yoyo*.

Day 4 (page 149)

1. yes /y/ /ĕ/ /s/
2. yum /y/ /ŭ/ /m/
3. yak /y/ /ă/ /k/
4. yell /y/ /ĕ/ /l/

Day 5 (page 150)

1. yam /y/ /ă/ /m/
2. yawn /y/ /ŏ/ /n/
3. yoga /y/ /ō/ /g/ /ə/
4. yoyo /y/ /ō/ /y/ /ō/

Week 28

Day 1 (page 151)

Day 2 (page 152)

Day 3 (page 153)

Students should color *koala* and *kangaroo*.

Day 4 (page 154)

1. dot /d/ /ŏ/ /t/
2. dig /d/ /ĭ/ /g/
3. dad /d/ /ă/ /d/

Day 5 (page 155)

1. yes /y/ /ĕ/ /s/
2. yolk /y/ /ō/ /k/
3. yam /y/ /ă/ /m/

Answer Key (cont.)

Unit 6

Week 29

Day 1 (page 157)

Listen for students identifying the /ĕ/ sound.

Day 2 (page 158)

The pictures are *elevator*, *sock*, *lobster*, and *bag*. Students should circle *elevator*.

Day 3 (page 159)

The first set of pictures are *calendar*, *bow*, *gloves*, and *egg*. Students should circle *egg*.

The second set of pictures are *flag*, *envelope*, and *door*. Students should color *envelope*.

Day 4 (page 160)

1. hen /h/ /ĕ/ /n/
2. bed /b/ /ĕ/ /d/
3. net /n/ /ĕ/ /t/
4. ten /t/ /ĕ/ /n/

Day 5 (page 161)

1. pen /p/ /ĕ/ /n/
2. web /w/ /ĕ/ /b/
3. jet /j/ /ĕ/ /t/
4. bell /b/ /ĕ/ /l/

Week 30

Day 1 (page 162)

Listen for students identifying the /qu/ sound.

Day 2 (page 163)

The pictures are *soap*, *quarter*, *piano*, and *kiwi*. Students should circle *quarter*.

Day 3 (page 164)

The first set of pictures are *bath*, *question*, *mug*, and *leaf*. Students should circle *question*.

The second set of pictures are *quail*, *book*, and *drum*. Students should color *quail*.

Day 4 (page 165)

1. quilt /qu/ /ilt/
2. queen /qu/ /een/
3. quiet /qu/ /iet/
4. quail /qu/ /ail/

Day 5 (page 166)

1. quill /qu/ /ill/
2. quiz /qu/ /iz/
3. quarter /qu/ /arter/
4. question /qu/ /estion/

Week 31

Day 1 (page 167)

Listen for students identifying the /w/ sound.

Day 2 (page 168)

The pictures are *seed*, *plum*, *cake*, and *whale*. Students should circle *whale*.

Day 3 (page 169)

The first set of pictures are *watermelon*, *fly*, *glass*, and *duck*. Students should circle *watermelon*.

The second set of pictures are *dollar*, *whistle*, and *boat*. Students should color *whistle*.

Day 4 (page 170)

1. web /w/ /ĕ/ /b/
2. wag /w/ /ă/ /g/
3. wake /w/ /ā/ /k/
4. win /w/ /ĭ/ /n/

Day 5 (page 171)

1. wig /w/ /ĭ/ /g/
2. wave /w/ /ā/ /v/
3. wall /w/ /ŏ/ /l/
4. week /w/ /ē/ /k/

Week 32

Day 1 (page 172)

Listen for students identifying the /v/ sound.

Day 2 (page 173)

The pictures are *vacuum*, *potato*, *flute*, and *button*. Students should circle *vacuum*.

Day 3 (page 174)

The first set of pictures are *lighthouse*, *queen*, *waffle*, and *vase*. Students should circle *vase*.

The second set of pictures are *yoyo*, *volcano*, and *cat*. Students should color *volcano*.

Answer Key (cont.)

Day 4 (page 175)

1. van /v/ /ă/ /n/
2. vet /v/ /ĕ/ /t/
3. cave /c/ /ā/ /v/
4. hive /h/ /ī/ /v/

Day 5 (page 176)

1. vase /v/ /ā/ /s/
2. vine /v/ /ī/ /n/
3. wave /w/ /ā/ /v/
4. dove /d/ /ŭ/ /v/

Week 33

Day 1 (page 177)

Listen for students identifying the /x/ and /z/ sounds.

Day 2 (page 178)

The pictures are *car*, *ax*, *goat*, and *cup*. Students should circle *ax*.

Day 3 (page 179)

The pictures are *zoo*, *barn*, *log*, and *olive*. Students should circle *zoo*.

Day 4 (page 180)

1. fix /f/ /ĭ/ /x/
2. box /b/ /ŏ/ /x/
3. zip /z/ /ĭ/ /p/
4. zoom /z/ /ōō/ /m/

Day 5 (page 181)

1. mix /m/ /ĭ/ /x/
2. fox /f/ /ŏ/ /x/
3. zero /z/ /ē/ /r/ /ō/
4. maze /m/ /ā/ /z/

Week 34

Day 1 (page 182)

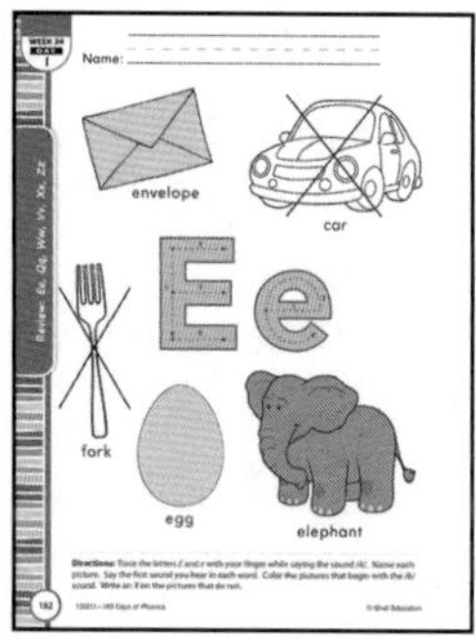

Day 2 (page 183)

Day 3 (page 184)

Students should color *wheel* and *window*.

Day 4 (page 185)

1. van /v/ /ă/ /n/
2. vet /v/ /ĕ/ /t/
3. vest /v/ /ĕ/ /s/ /t/

Day 5 (page 186)

1. fox /f/ /ŏ/ /x/
2. zip /z/ /ĭ/ /p/

Unit 7

Week 35

Day 1 (page 188)

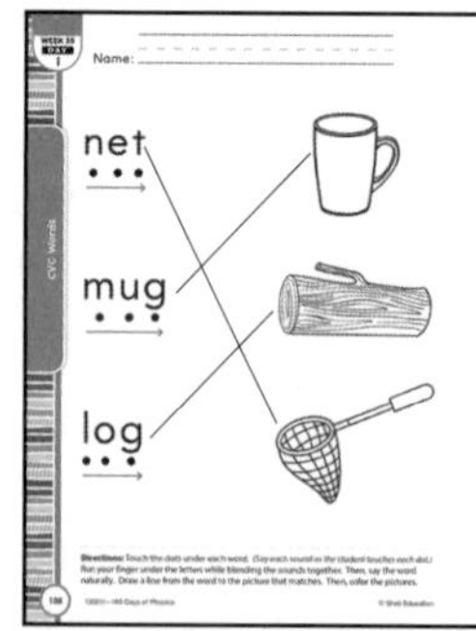

Day 2 (page 189)

1. web
2. map
3. sad
4. rug

Answer Key *(cont.)*

Day 3 (page 190)

1. rat
2. fan
3. leg
4. zip

Day 4 (page 191)

sun

Day 5 (page 192)

1. mat
2. sub
3. van
4. nut

Week 36

Day 1 (page 193)

Day 2 (page 194)

1. pot
2. nap
3. mom
4. hat

Day 3 (page 195)

1. pan
2. bug
3. fox
4. cot

Day 4 (page 196)

pig

Day 5 (page 197)

1. bat
2. dog
3. top
4. bed

Digital Resources

Accessing the Digital Resources

The digital resources can be downloaded by following these steps:

1. Go to **www.tcmpub.com/digital**
2. Use the 13-digit ISBN number to redeem the digital resources.
3. Respond to the questions using the book.
4. Follow the prompts on the Content Cloud website to sign in or create a new account.
5. The content redeemed will now be on your My Content screen. Click on the product to look through the digital resources. All resources are available for download. Select files can be previewed, opened, and shared.

For questions and assistance with your ISBN redemption, please contact Teacher Created Materials.

email: customerservice@tcmpub.com

phone: 800-858-7339

Contents of the Digital Resources

- Standards Correlations
- Class and Individual Analysis Sheets
- Hands-On Letter Practice
- Writing Practice

Notes